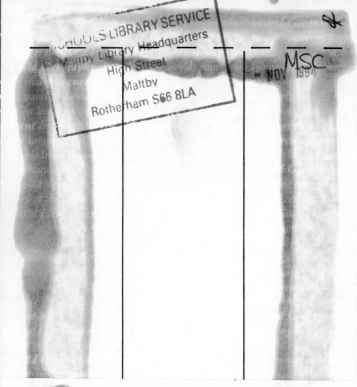

FALLOW COMBINE HARVESTER ARABLE GRAIN BEEF FARMING DAIRY FARMING FEEDLOTS HUNTING & GATHERING THRESHING

SHEEP FARMING WHEAT YARD FARMING PIGS CROCODILES INDUSTRIAL CROPS FRUIT MAIZE RICE COLLECTIVE PLANTATION

World Geography

Farms

& the world's food supply

Atlantic Europe Publishing

How to use this book

There are many ways of using this book. Below you will see how each page is arranged to help you to find information quickly, revise main ideas or look for material in detail. The choice is yours!

On some pages you will find words that have been shown in CAPITALS. There is a full explanation of each of these words in the glossary on page 63.

This heading in the running text tells you about the section that follows.

This is the main column of running text that forms the chapter. Read this for a good understanding of the subject as a whole.

Scan these boxes for key ideas.

The information in the box describes an important subject in detail and gives additional facts.

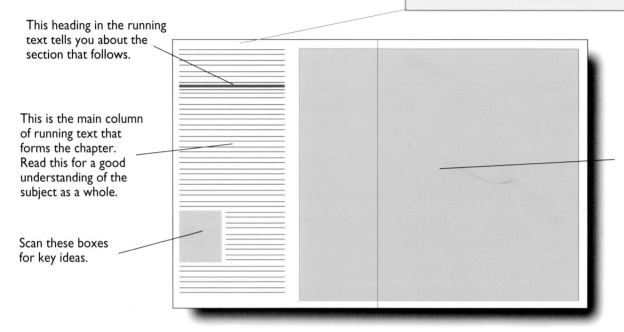

Author
Brian Knapp, BSc, PhD
Educational Consultant
Stephen Codrington, BSc, PhD
Art Director
Duncan McCrae, BSc
Editor
Elizabeth Walker, BA
Illustrator
David Woodroffe
Designed and produced by
EARTHSCAPE EDITIONS
Print consultants
Landmark Production Consultants Ltd
Printed and bound by
Paramount Printing Company Ltd

First published in the United Kingdom in 1994 by Atlantic Europe Publishing Company Limited, 86 Peppard Road, Sonning Common, Reading, Berkshire, RG4 9RP, UK

Copyright © 1994
Atlantic Europe Publishing Company Limited

The Atlantic Europe Publishing logo is a registered trademark of Atlantic Europe Publishing Company Limited.

Suggested cataloguing location

Knapp, Brian
    Farms & the world's food supply
    – (World Geography; 6)
630

ISBN 1-869860-58-6

Acknowledgements
The publishers would like to thank the following for their help and advice: *Aspen Flying Club,* Englewood, Colorado; *Baramundi Air,* Cairns, Queensland; *Terry Barringer,* Royal Commonwealth Society Library, Cambridge University; *Stephen and Penny Bitmead and Andrew Carr* of Bitmead Estates; *Bendigo Aviation Services,* Bendigo, VIC, Australia; *Bridgeford Flying Service,* Napa, California; *Matthew Cherian,* Oxfam-Bridge, India; *Duncan and Jeane Cooper; Eveland Aero,* Honolulu, Hawaii; *David Newell,* Oxfam-Bridge, Thailand; *Audrey and Kah-Tin Teoh,* Ka kang, Malaysia.

Picture credits
(c=centre t=top b=bottom l=left r=right)
All photographs are from the **Earthscape Editions** library except the following: **Stephen Codrington** 11tr, 33t; **Jack Jackson** 13t, 17b, 20/21; **Panos Picture Library** 59b (*Penny Tweedie*), 27 (*Ron Giling*), 34/35 (*Jim Holmes*); **Royal Commonwealth Society Library** 27b; **The Sutcliffe Gallery** 18/19, 23tr; **University of Reading, Rural History Centre** 22bl, 22tr, 23cr, 25t, 28/29, 56bl; **Tony Waltham** 24tl, 32b, 33b and **Zefa** 21t.

This product is manufactured from sustainable managed forests. For every tree cut down at least one more is planted.

Contents

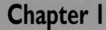
Facts about farming

Farming provides food – our most basic need – and farmers are our most essential workers.

Of the world's five and a half billion people, three quarters still farm and depend directly on their farms to survive. In the DEVELOPING WORLD more families still depend on farming than on all other kinds of work combined.

But although farming is no less important to the industrial world, it has taken a different route. Fewer than one in twenty work the land, and farming has become a world of giant machines.

It may seem strange to us today, but in the last century there were still fields in most of the world's big cities. Land was needed to graze the horses that pulled carts and carriages. Many of the poor grew their own vegetables. Many others went on seasonal trips from the city to help gather in the harvests in the country. Even fresh milk came from herds of cows that were housed in city dairies. And human and animal waste went back from the cities to fertilise the fields.

Today the connections between city and country are far weaker. Refrigeration and fast

❏ (left) Waiting at a market, these sheep are gathered by their thousand from the nearby rangeland where they graze in traditional fashion.

But as populations grow and shoppers seek lower prices for their food, more and more pressure is placed on farmland and farmers.
The task facing farmers worldwide is to get the most from the land at the lowest cost, to treat animals with respect, and to preserve the land for future generations. It is becoming an ever-greater challenge.

transport allows fresh produce to reach the shops quickly. But the link between city and country needs to remain strong; we all need food to eat, and the majority of it must come from farms.

Farms, of course, provide much more than food. They can provide fibres such as wool and cotton, vegetable oil for many products such as soaps, and even the fuel for some of the world's automobiles.

> Customers unknowingly begin to place demands on farmers. These demands can cause widespread harm in the countryside.

But as farmers and customers in industrial countries become separated, customers – unknowingly – begin to place demands on the price and the quality of the produce, which can cause widespread harm in the countryside. Farming could become dangerously out of balance with the natural environment. If this is to be prevented then everyone needs to understand the nature of the world's farms and the world's food supply.

The principles of farming

Put yourself in the place of a farmer who must use the resources of water, soil, plants and animals and the energy from sunshine to provide food to sell. And yet the soil must be left in good shape for the generations to follow.

The goal of farming should be to provide food that gives a balanced, healthy diet for all. To succeed in this farmers have to have probably the broadest knowledge of all workers. A farmer has to mix an understanding of the environment (such as the climate and the soil) and a knowledge of plants and animals, with a mechanic's knowledge of how machines work and the shopkeeper's experience of what customers want.

Nature provides the countryside

The farming system

Although there are many ways, or systems, of farming in the world, all farmers have to work with the resources of the soil and climate.

As far as the environment allows, farmers can choose whether to produce plants or animals, and which methods of farming they want to use.

Successful farming produces a yield from the farm. Subsistence farmers use this to live on; commercial farmers use part of the profit to buy more fertiliser, pay wages, and buy machinery, seed and new animals.

This pattern of using the land is called the farming system.

Because there are so many things involved, there is no easy formula in farming, no single right way to succeed. That is why there have been such different ways of farming in the past and why there are still so many ways of farming today.

It is also the reason why some farming methods are suited to the needs of the people and the environment, whereas others are, in the long run, quite unsuitable. If a farmer puts back into the system (in the form of manure, artificial fertilisers and good management) at least as much as he takes out, then the land can be farmed for ever. If the farmer takes more from the land than he returns, then the land will suffer and eventually become useless.

The natural resources of the land

Farmers adapt the countryside to provide food. Much of the natural world has already been replaced by farmland. However, crops still depend on nourishment from the soil and on sunshine, rain, and warmth provided by the climate, just as wild plants did in the past. This means that farmers have to work within strict natural rules.

Farmers work the land

2 The means of farming

Despite thousands of years of experimenting, only about two hundred plants and fifty animal species have been adapted for farming.

The most useful plants are the grains (wheat, maize, rice, etc.) which are all derived from wild grasses. All domesticated animals depend on grasses or other plants for their food.

The domesticated animals with the greatest meat yield are pigs and cattle.

The way that plants grow cannot easily be hurried. This is why the farmer's year is a cycle of ploughing, planting and harvesting that follows the seasons.

Shoppers buy the produce

3 Food for customers

The products of the farms find their way to markets and shops. By the way we shop, we force farmers to produce cheaper food, with a higher quality, better looks and more even size and shape than ever before.

Here are some of the pressures we put on farmers:

☛ Our demand for cheap, plentiful food can cause farmers to overwork the soil, destroy forests and hedges (thus destroying the environment of wildlife), and over-use fertilisers so that the excess seeps into rivers.

☛ Our demand for foods such as lean meat and rosy tomatoes causes plants and animals to be bred simply to make our tables look nice.

☛ Our demand for cheap coffee, tea, cocoa and sugar can cause land in distant countries to be used for our crops rather than to meet the needs of the local people.

☛ To earn a reasonable living, farmers are forced to demand help from government (called **SUBSIDIES**) which we then pay for through taxes.

☛ Over-subsidising farmers can produce surpluses which have to be stored because they cannot be sold.

Many ways to farm

The natural regions of the world vary with rainfall and temperature. This produces a wide range of regions from tropical rainforest, savanna, desert, deciduous forest and steppe grassland to coniferous forest and tundra.

Farmers have to decide how to adapt this natural world. Because they make different decisions, the result is a chequerboard of uses as shown in the panel on the right.

Here you can see that farmers can choose how intensively they want to use the land:

☛ They can use the land as it is, perhaps for grazing sheep or cattle. This a low-use way to farm.

☛ They can add fertilisers and water, or help the plants or animals in other ways. This is a moderate or high-use way to farm.

The first way costs the least money, but the second way gives more food.

The farming 'chequerboard'

If you look at this chequerboard you will see that it is arranged in rows and columns. Each row relates to a particular type of climate. The climate sets the scene.

In each row there are three kinds of choice: to farm without altering the land very much (extensive farming), to make a moderate amount of alteration to the land, and finally to make large changes in order to squeeze as much from the land as possible (intensive farming).

What kind of system a farmer chooses depends on how much money he has to buy machinery, fertilisers, etc., and how much land the farmer has.

Farmers with large areas of land often farm extensively because they can get a good living without too many changes. On the other hand, farmers who must make a living from a small area nearly always farm intensively.

In recent years there has been considerable outcry at the nature of intensive rearing, especially for chickens and pigs. As a result more people choose, for example, to buy free range eggs and poultry. This is forcing some change on the farmers, as consumers are prepared to pay more for giving animals a higher quality of life.

❐ (above) Intensive rice growing using terraces.

❐ (right) Extensive cereal growing on flat land. In this case the fields are used to grow a variety of crops, which is the reason the fields appear different colours.

❐ (right) A large intensive livestock unit. The animals are kept indoors throughout their lives and are fed on a mixture of cereals and enriched foods.

	The natural world	Low use	Moderate use	High use
Polar regions	Tundra is at the limit of plant growth. More animals survive in the oceans than on land. The total plant and animal matter on land is small.	Hunting and gathering is the main way of survival.	There is no moderate use of these lands	There is no intensive use of these lands
Temperate regions	The coniferous forest region has long, snowy winters with frozen soils. The wildlife needs special adaptations to the climate and the growing season is short.	Traditional herding. Migrating animals are most important.	Grazing of cleared land, Dairy and beef cattle. Transhumance.	There is no intensive use of these lands
Temperate regions	The deciduous rainforest grades into grasslands (prairies/steppes) away from the oceans. Warm summers provide a good growing season, rainfall is moderate and rarely causes erosion.	Nomadic herding in areas like the steppes.	Traditional use of land in wetter regions in mixed family farms which aim to balance crops and animals. Dry grasslands are used as range for beef cattle and sheep.	Crop-growing, huge cereal farms; some animals.
Deserts	Deserts have sparse and unreliable rainfall. All plants and animals are adapted to cope with the lack of food and water.	Hunter-gatherers, such as the Kalahari bushmen, make use of adapted plants and animals.	There is no moderate use of these lands	Market garden crops rely on irrigation.
Deserts	Savanna: hot all year; long dry season; long wet season, with torrential rain.	Nomadic herders and shifting cultivation for growing crops.	Rangelands for beef cattle and sheep.	Irrigation for plantations and rice paddies.
Tropical regions	The equatorial region has hot, humid conditions all year. Very high rainfall, poor soils.	Hunter-gatherers rely on the natural supply of food from native plants.	Tree plantations and cattle ranches. (Cattle ranches fail wherever they are established).	Paddy fields for rice and crop plantations.

Many choices in grazing

Grazing is one of the two main types of farming. The farmers who rear animals in this way are called pastoralists. Because grazing animals can eat natural grasses, the main task of these farmers is, therefore, to find fresh supplies of pasture.

One solution is to develop a special way of life, constantly moving from one place to another in search of the best grasses. Such people are called nomadic herders, and their life is spent living in temporary camps along the route they follow during a year.

> Herding is a system usually found where crops cannot be grown.

Nomadic herding depends on a close relationship between people and animals. People have to look after their animals constantly, protecting them from wild animals or thieves and guiding them from one pasture to another.

An alternative is called ranching, and it is used in the open plains of Australia and the Americas as well as in the hills and mountains of Europe. Ranch animals are branded and

(above) These sheep in England are fenced in; if they were in India they would be tended constantly by their owners.

'Extensive' ways of grazing

On land that has a long dry season, as well as on land that is cool and rainy, it is often impossible to grow crops. It would not even pay to add fertiliser and try to improve the land. In these places farmers often use the land as range, allowing livestock to graze over large areas.

The age-old way of rangeland grazing uses many people. Every herd is tended by its owners. As the cattle wander across the landscape finding food, the people follow. In areas with a big contrast between seasons, the way many people coped was to be constantly on the move to fresh pastures. These people became nomads.

But there is another way to farm the same lands. Ranchers put barbed wire fences across the range. Each area of range keeps only as many animals as can find enough food for themselves throughout the year.

The main difference between these methods is that traditional farming costs less but uses many more people; the modern method costs more money for fencing, but fewer people have to be paid.

Both these ways of farming are known as extensive farming.

Ranches and rangeland

Dryland pastures or ranches – called rangelands in America and outback in Australia – occur in the near-desert (semi-arid) centres of many continents. Mid-latitude rangelands are especially harsh environments for farmers because, in addition to lack of water, they have searingly hot summers (up to 40 °C) and bitterly cold winters (down to -40 °C), conditions which tax even the hardiest beef cattle. Typical temperate grasses are tough and wiry and are not very nutritious.

It is often impossible to support even one animal per hectare of range.

(below) A ranch in Texas (USA).

Sheep and the outback

The dry grass and shrublands of Australia are called the outback. Like all dry grasslands, they can support only the hardiest of animals and at very low densities. This is why Australian outback farmers have traditionally reared sheep. A water supply for the animals is a major consideration for farmers where rainfall is so unreliable. The Great Artesian Basin, which lies to the west of the Great Dividing Range, can be tapped for its underground water. Although the water is quite salty, and therefore unsuited to irrigating crops, animals can drink it without problems. Farmers set up small wind-operated pumps to supply watering troughs across their land. This allows the animals to range over the entire farm rather than having to concentrate near a few watering places.

Nomadic herders

The word nomad comes from a Greek word meaning pasture. The majority of nomadic people are herders, and in that sense they are farmers, caring for domesticated sheep, goats, camels and cattle.

Nomadic people still live in areas where it would be impossible to settle permanently, such as Central Asia (the dry Steppes and the Gobi desert) and Africa south of the Sahara desert.

Nomads move with the seasons. In central Asia, for example, nomads move north in the summer to grazing areas that have been snowbound throughout the winter; in winter they move south to escape the harshest weather and to use the grass that has grown during the summer. In Africa, nomadic peoples like the Fulani (Nigeria) and the Masai (Kenya) move north and then south each year, following the path of the rains.

❒ (below) Rangeland cattle in Australia.

then allowed to wander freely and find their own grazing land within limits set by barbed-wire fences. They are gathered up – corralled – just once a year, and some animals are sent for slaughter or their fleeces sheared, as appropriate.

Ranching does not necessarily produce a greater yield of meat per animal than herding, but fewer people are needed, so the return for each farm worker is much higher. It is best suited to areas where wild animals and the risk of theft has been largely removed.

But the land can be used more intensively. Grass can be irrigated so that it will grow faster, and more animals can then be kept on the land. Alternatively animals can be grazed on some fields while others are used to grow extra food – fodder – which can be harvested and stored for use in the months when natural grazing is scarce.

The most intensive of all types of animal farming is to keep animals in stalls or pens. They are fed with cereals and grass from the fields around, and with a selection of special foods to make them grow very fast.

Choices in growing crops

People who choose to grow crops need a fertile soil, good moisture in the growing season and sunny warm conditions later in the year to allow the seed to ripen. Areas with poor soils, unreliable rainfall or which are very humid are not really suitable for crops.

> Growing cereals is the most efficient system of farming.

Shifting cultivation is a traditional method of allowing nature to replace nourishment that is taken from the soil by crops, but it relies on large amounts of surplus land. In this system fields are cultivated until the plants yield poorly. They are then abandoned and new fields are made in the wilderness. Thus by shifting about people can better rely on crops year after year.

Shifting cultivation

The first objective of the majority of the world's farmers is to grow enough food to feed their families. They are self-sufficient farmers.

Self-sufficient farmers (sometimes called subsistence farmers) need to know how much food to grow, and perhaps how many animals to keep. They need to find ways of storing food or having it fresh every day, and they need to ensure that the food will give a balanced, healthy diet.

How a farmer can achieve self-sufficiency depends on the land and the climate, and the farms that result can be extremely varied. In general, smallholders do not have the money to be able to pay for food if their own harvests fail. As insurance, therefore, they grow a variety of crops. Thus the farmer insures a harvest even if one crop fails due to weather, disease or pests.

This form of farming is very well adapted to get the most from the environment, but it uses large amounts of labour (it is labour-intensive) and is not suited to the use of machines or to getting surplus produce to market quickly.

❏ (right) An illustration of shifting cultivation as practised in Africa.

Shifting cultivation

Shifting cultivation is a way of cultivating land for crops that has developed in many parts of the world. It relies on the way the land can revitalise itself after cropping.

A village of farmers will burn a patch of scrub or forest and chop down any remaining unburned tree stumps. The cleared ground is then planted with seed.

When the seeds begin to grow, the ash from the burned vegetation acts as a fertiliser, giving the young plants a good start. When the crop is harvested, the ground is planted again, ready for the next harvest.

Soils have a natural store of nourishment that is gradually used up as each crop is harvested and carried away. After four or five years, the store of nourishment is almost entirely exhausted and so crops grow less and less well. At this stage the farmers move to a new patch of land and begin to clear this in turn.

While crops are growing in the newly cleared land, the abandoned field gradually becomes overgrown with wild plants. This allows the soil to begin a slow recovery, building up a new store of nourishment which can support plants in the future. It may, however, take thirty to fifty years before the exhausted field has built up its store of nourishment again, so the farmers must shift from plot to plot in the meantime.

Shifting cultivation uses from five to ten times as much land as farming using artificial fertilisers. But because no artificial fertilisers are needed, it is a vastly more economical way of farming for people with low incomes.

Problems with shifting cultivation

Land used for shifting cultivation can be abused when people become trapped into reusing their land too quickly. This can happen in places where populations are increasing rapidly.

Farms become smaller as land is divided among heirs on the death of the farmer. As a result land is often reused before it has had time to recover from an earlier use, and the yield of crops is lower than it should be.

Soil that is used too soon and too often is also vulnerable to soil erosion. Millions of hectares of the region called the Sahel, south of the Sahara in Africa, are being over-used in this way.

In places such as Southeast Asia, where shifting cultivation occurs in forest lands, large areas of forest are being destroyed. This leaves the soil exposed to rain erosion which may help cause flooding in low-lying regions.

❐ (above) A simple plough being used for cultivation. Many farms are still worked by hoe without any help from animals.

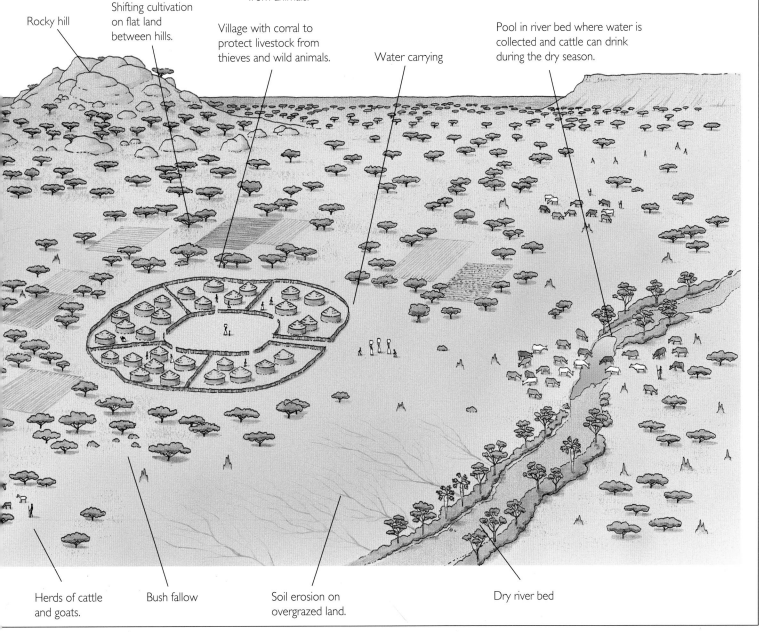

Rocky hill

Shifting cultivation on flat land between hills.

Village with corral to protect livestock from thieves and wild animals.

Water carrying

Pool in river bed where water is collected and cattle can drink during the dry season.

Herds of cattle and goats.

Bush fallow

Soil erosion on overgrazed land.

Dry river bed

A more intensive way of using the land is to 'rest' it from cereals but still use the soil. This is a system called rotation. In this system, a grain crop might be planted for three to five years and then replaced with a crop such as a root vegetable that takes different kinds of nourishment from the soil.

> Mixed farming helps a farmer to spread the risk of crop failure and to find a use for many kinds of soil.

The most intensive use of the land is to grow cereals year after year. The world's best cereal-growing lands - the North American prairies in particular - make the best use of the large, efficient machinery that is now available to the cereal farmer. So rotation has often been replaced by the use of artificial fertilisers and pesticides.

Choices in mixed farming

Traditionally people farmed so they could be at least self-sufficient. They had to plan a balance of many different ways of getting food. This is why so many traditional systems had a mixture of cereals, vegetables and animals.

These farms were developed on the principle that if one kind of farming failed then there were others that would probably succeed. The farmer chose a balanced system of moderate land use.

Mixed systems used on general farms allowed the plant remains from crops to be fed to animals and for the animal manure to be used to fertilise the cropland. But crops were not grown on a large scale and animals were only reared in small numbers, so they could never be the cheapest way of producing food. This is why a general farm is the choice of fewer farmers today.

Farming with irrigation

Irrigation – adding extra water to fields – allows crops to be harvested where the rainfall is unreliable, or during a dry season.

For example, across North America water is pumped from underground water-bearing rocks (AQUIFERS). Pumps are connected to long booms that can move in a circle and sprinkle water to a large area of ground.

Some crops, such as rice, cannot be grown unless the ground is flooded. This is why most rice is grown on land beside rivers throughout East Asia, the world's main rice-growing area.

Since ancient times, irrigation canals have been built to carry water from rivers or springs to the fields. But this form of irrigation can be very wasteful of water, and today it is possible to use sprays or sprinklers to scatter water across the crops much in the same fashion as rainfall.

The problem is that as more and more land is used for crops, even more water is needed. In many areas almost all the surplus water is now used up.

❏ (below) Fruit trees being irrigated by flood irrigation. When orchards are flooded in this way, a large amount of water is lost by EVAPORATION. But fruit trees do not need to be in flooded ground. Modern systems of pipes carry water to the plant roots and save huge amounts of water.

Ancient irrigation methods

The most famous early world civilisation – the ancient Egyptians – lived in a desert. But they were immensely successful cultivators because they farmed on the delta of the Nile. The yearly flood from the river brought nourishment to the fields, and soaked the soils long enough for an entire crop to grow. As a result the Egyptians produced large crops of wheat, as well as flax for fibres. In the Indus valley of South Asia there was similar success from natural flood waters, with wheat, rice, cotton and sugar cane.

In the dry areas of North America the need for settled farming became severe about 3000 years ago, and it was then that maize was domesticated. Again it was most successful in areas such as near present day Mexico City where lake waters provided constant moisture for the crops.

Some places were less favoured, however. In the Iranian desert, long tunnels, crossing many tens of kilometres, were dug to carry water from springs in the mountains to the fields near the villages. In the South America, irrigation canals carried water across the slopes of the Andes mountains. And in vast areas of Asia, irrigation provided water to the rice crops.

❐ (above) In places where central pivot irrigation is common, the view from the air is very strange. Here you can see a huge area of fields irrigated by booms and sprinklers.

❐ (above) In this close up view of a central pivot irrigation system you can clearly see the boom that carries the water sprinklers. The boom is fixed to a pump in the centre of the field which draws water from underground.

❐ (above) Spray irrigation is much less wasteful of water than flooding. These peanuts, for example, thrive better on sprinkler water than if the ground were flooded.

❐ (above) Flooding rice fields is essential because rice is a marsh plant that will only grow properly in waterlogged ground.

Making use of difficult environments

Some of the most difficult problems that farmers have to cope with are drought, harsh winters and steeply sloping land.

Drought is a particular concern to farmers where the rainfall naturally varies greatly from year to year. Here the only way to make sure a crop thrives is to use water from rivers or from rocks underground. But adding water – irrigation – is expensive and many farmers therefore choose to use the land (less heavily) for animal range.

For farmers who live in hilly and mountainous regions the problem is how to make the land suitable for farming at all. Many hill farmers have laboriously made terraces across the steepest land.

Mountain lands present many difficulties for the farmer, especially in winter. At high altitudes, and with cloudy skies and frequent rainfall in summer, crops will not ripen and farmers are forced to raise livestock. In winter the land is completely snowbound.

Even animal farming is difficult in the high valleys and if farmers are to make a living from the short growing season they need to use every small scrap of land. They do this by moving animals from one pasture to another with the seasons. This is called transhumance.

Transhumance

Transhumance is an age-old way of getting the most from mountain land. As soon as the snows clear on the upper slopes, animals that have been kept indoors all winter are taken to the high pastures. During the summer the valley bottom pastures are used to grow hay for animal feed during the next winter.

The upland pastures are not fenced. Traditionally children and old people tend the animals and live in châlets on the high pastures throughout the snow-free months. However, although this system is still worked in places like the Himalayas, the pressures of schooling and modern life have meant it is now very rare in the European Alps or Scandinavian mountains.

❐ (left and below) The landscape of transhumance in the European Alps.

| In late spring, as soon as the snow melts, cattle are taken to high pastures to graze.

2 During the short summer farmers grow fodder crops and cut grass for hay from the valley meadows.

3 By early Autumn snow begins to fall on the high slopes and the cattle must return to their indoor shelter.

4 During the winter the farms are snowbound and the villages cut off.

Terracing and soil conservation

With the growth of the world's population, many steeply sloping lands are now being brought into cultivation for the first time. But in countries where thunderstorms produce heavy rainfall, even moderate slopes can quickly become eroded if they are left bare.

One way to cultivate slopes is to form terraces. In the past terraces were made by building stone walls, but this was very time-consuming. A simple way to terrace the land quickly is to dig a trench across the slope and pile the soil on the upslope side (see the picture on the right). The idea is to provide a place where water will pond up during a rainstorm. In such ponds, soil can settle out of the water, and the water is given more time to seep into the hillside.

❒ (left) Digging new terraces on eroded land is not easy. It needs teamwork and back-breaking effort. But eventually the land will be able to support more crops.

❒ (below) An immense amount of effort was applied to these slopes in Yemen centuries ago. These slopes would have been too steep to farm in any other way.

Chapter 2

Revolutions in farming

Today farmers in many countries are caught up in the race to produce more and more food.

But the need for change is nothing new. It dates back to over 28,000 years ago when the first farmers gave up trying to feed themselves from wild plants and began tilling their land.

Ever since, farmers have had to struggle harder and harder to squeeze more and more food from the land.

To our early ancestors, the Earth was a land of plenty. It provided them with a natural food supply throughout the year and, although they may have had to move from place to place with the seasons, they were able to gather fruits, nuts, tubers and many other kinds of food. Occasionally they would also have been able to hunt or trap a wild animal.

People who collect their food from the natural environment – we often mistakenly call it 'wilderness' – are called hunter-gatherers. They practise a very economical way of 'farming' in terms of effort because the land does not have to be worked nor the animals tended.

However, food is spread thinly in a natural environment and just a few people may need to 'own' large areas if they are to collect enough

❒ (left) Farming before the age of powered machines was a matter of working on a small scale and making the most of human labour. Everywhere people were general mixed farmers. As a result, even in the most advanced nations at least half the people worked in the fields.

food for their needs. This is the reason hunter-gatherer peoples always have been scattered in small groups.

The need to farm

Hunters and gatherers became cultivators and herders more out of necessity than choice. After all, it is much harder to till the land or to tend animals than it is to go out and collect what nature has provided.

If you are a farmer, you are tied to the land you work, often seven days a week, year in, year out.

However, the option of simply gathering what nature provides did not exist where the numbers of people grew large. The stark choice facing many of our ancestors was therefore either to starve or to find ways of providing more food than the environment would naturally provide.

> Hunting and gathering uses far less effort than any farm system, but it only works where land is plentiful.

As a result, generation after generation of people have been obliged to learn ways to domesticate (or husband) animals, or clear ground and grow edible plants (or crops). In this way they became farmers.

Early farmers

The progress of cultivation or the domestication of animals charts the time and place where people outgrew the natural resources of the land.

☛ In the Solomon Islands of the Pacific, where great expanses of ocean prevent people from spreading out and colonising new land easily, there are signs that the people had reached the limits of gathering some 28,000 years ago and had turned to cultivation.

☛ In the dry lands of the Middle East, where naturally edible plants are few, quite sophisticated cultivation began about 10,000 years ago.

Hunting and gathering

Farming is not always the best way to use the land. In many areas the climate or the soil makes farming impossible. In the tropical rainforests, for example, it is difficult to find crops that will produce good yields year after year.

Unless there are vital reasons to farm, therefore, it is sensible to use the fruits of the natural trees and other plants which are adapted to the environment.

In dry environments such as deserts, farming can only be achieved with enormous amounts of irrigation. But wild plants can survive and be harvested from even these hostile conditions, as the Kalahari bushmen (San people) of Africa and Aboriginal Australians discovered many thousands of years ago.

In cold environments, such as the Arctic, crops cannot be relied upon because the summer growing season is so short. During the winter it may be impossible to find enough food to

keep domesticated animals in corrals. In these cases it makes sense to cull some wild animals such as moose and bear during the summer season, and leave others to survive through the winter.

Too many people searching the same area for food soon over-use the natural food supplies.

❑ (right) Small tribal groups still manage to live undisturbed in the depths of the rainforests of South America. This apparently lush forest contains a quite small amount of food, and each group needs a large area of forest for its survival.

❑ (below) Inuit (Eskimo) people had to develop their food gathering to match the harsh environment. They almost exclusively hunted and fished because there is very little nourishment in the plants that grow in the Arctic.

Preservation techniques include salting and curing food. During the long winters the food is naturally in deep freeze.

☛ In China and Southeast Asia rice paddy farming was well established 8000 years ago and fields terraced up steep slopes.

☛ In Europe cultivation was not needed until about 5000 years ago.

☛ In the Andes mountains, native people learned to cultivate potatoes, terrace land and irrigate their crops over 3000 years ago.

Many traditional ways of working the land used large numbers of people.

☛ In the plains of North America, Africa and Australia, where there were fewer people and almost limitless amounts of food, farming was not needed at all until the people of European descent arrived with their demands to feed people in distant markets.

The Age of Discovery

By about the 15th century, farming was an ancient and varied way of making a living throughout the world. The most favoured areas were the tropical and near-tropical regions of Asia, where a wide range of crops could be cultivated with ease.

Europeans looked on these lands of variety with envy, and expeditions sailed to buy the spices needed to flavour the plain (and often putrefying) European food.

In Europe farming was especially hard. The climate is cool and wet and the soil heavy. It would grow only a limited range of crops, and yields were low.

❏ (above) A 14th century manuscript showing the traditional way of sowing seed – and the need to protect the crop from pests.

Development of farm implements

Farming has been revolutionised by many advances in TECHNOLOGY. The development of the plough, harrow, harvester and tractor have had profound effects on farming. Not only have they increased the productivity of farm workers, but they have allowed previously unworkable land to be brought into cultivation.

❑ (below) Traditional instruments, such as the plough, were continually being refined. People were proud of their new designs, as this 18th century painting shows.

❑ (below) By the middle of the 20th century tractors were able to plough land in a fraction of the time it took horses. The result was a dramatic loss in farming jobs.

❑ (left) By the end of the 19th century the horse-drawn plough was a well established method of tilling the land. However it was about to be replaced by tractors, and millions of horses would disappear from the farming landscape.

Cultivating

The earliest farming implements were hoes made of animal horns. Later curved iron boards were added to wooden handles so the hoe could be used with an overhead swinging motion.

This implement, known as the *jembi* in Africa, is still in wide use on smallholdings. To cultivate large areas, teams of people have to co-operate.

Animal power can be harnessed to allow a different sort of cultivating, known as ploughing. The earliest plough – known as a scratch plough – also used natural materials, such as an antler or a sharply pointed stick. These were fitted with handles to guide the tool, and some form of harness so that it could be pulled. The sharp end of the plough was dug into the soil and then pulled along, sometimes by people, mostly by animals such as oxen.

This simple plough broke up the soil in narrow lines, and it was used to make a criss-cross pattern over the field. But it was very light weight and really only suitable for dry, easily worked soils with little vegetation. So although it could be used in the dry lands of the Middle East and lands bordering the Mediterranean, for example, it was not strong enough to be used on the moist, heavy clay soils of Northern Europe.

In Europe a plough was developed with a curved blade (the mouldboard) to turn the soil over and a blade in the front (the coulter) to cut a path through the heavy soil.

Modern tractors can pull twenty ploughs at a time, at speeds of over ten kilometres an hour. In this way an area that once took a horse-drawn plough a day can be covered by a tractor-drawn plough in less than five minutes!

Harvesting

Harvesting involves a number of separate activities. The cereal has to be cut, the grain separated from the rest of the cereal plant and carried to a dry store, and the stalk carried away to make bedding for animals and a wide range of other uses.

The original tool for cutting the ripe crop – reaping – was the stone knife, but this was quickly replaced by a curved metal tool, the sickle. Sickles are still widely used today in the developing world.

Removing the grain from the cut plant – threshing – had traditionally been done by beating the cereal on the ground. Finally, carrying away the products of harvest was done by bullock cart.

A combine harvester can reap, thresh and bale up straw all in a single pass. Each machine may be able to harvest 50 ha. a day. This is equal to the toil of thousands of farm labourers working by hand.

Landlords made matters worse. They owned vast estates which were worked by armies of peasants who cultivated crops in large 'common' fields. But no matter how hard they tried, they only just provided enough for survival.

But Europe would change in a most dramatic way. In part this was through the Voyages of Discovery, and in part because the old system of landholding collapsed.

The more lands that fell under colonisation, the more trade became important. The New World of the Americas was a rich source of food and industrial crops, and they were quickly adopted in the Old World. Potatoes were brought from South America to Europe, coffee was taken from Africa to South America, maize was transferred between the Americas. And so the list went on.

During the Age of Discovery new crops were transferred between continents and new worlds of farming possibilities were opened up.

The period after Columbus saw new waves of farming revolutions, spreading the world with new crops and new ways of cultivating them. At the same time there were great changes in society, so that many traditional ways of life collapsed, and, most profound of all, the INDUSTRIAL REVOLUTION began.

Plantations

The farms that were opened up by trading companies in the colonies were completely revolutionary. They were on a giant scale never seen before.

The reason for the large farms was that Europeans were especially interested in large amounts of crops that would not thrive in Europe. The European powers soon established plantations throughout Africa, Asia, the Pacific, the Caribbean and Latin America. On these large landholdings, such cash crops as coffee,

Landlord and landless

The earliest farmers often owned their own land and had a choice of what they grew. But these were dangerous times for the individual farmer, who risked being killed by bandits just for his food. Often he and his family badly needed the protection of more powerful allies.

So gradually the small farmers gave away the rights to their land in exchange for protection from larger landlords. Eventually this gave rise to the system of farming called manorialism.

In the manorial system, which operated in Japan, India, China and throughout Europe, the land, which was known as the manor, was owned by a wealthy noble, known as a lord. Peasants worked in large open fields. As 'rent' for the use of the land, peasants were charged in farm produce, money and services. In return the lord of the manor provided protection and also kept a reserve amount of food which would be given out on credit to the peasants in years when the harvests failed.

The labourers, known as serfs, lived in small settlements close to the manor, and often near the manor house. Each serf farmed a set of strips on each of the three great manorial fields. By scattering the land farmed in this way, each serf would have a share of good and bad land.

❒ (above) These are tenant farmers in the 19th century. They had to work the land for as much produce as they could make, then pay a rent to their Scottish 'laird'.

Enclosed land

Farmland in much of the industrial world is enclosed by walls, wire fences or hedges. Enclosures were first introduced in Britain in the 17th century as a way of cutting the cost of farm labour. By enclosing fields there was no longer a need for people to accompany animals as they grazed.

Enclosed land could not be farmed communally, but had to be worked by a single farmer.

In the New World ranchers resisted enclosing the land and the battles between rancher and homesteaders – the Cattle Wars – were fierce. Today all of the American range is fenced.

Enclosures save on labour. As a shortage of people is not a problem in Asia or Africa, few fields are enclosed. Following tradition, animals graze on the verges of the fields tended by children and elderly people.

◻ (Below) Croft means 'enclosed field'. Crofts in Scotland developed as a special type of manorial pattern. When old common lands were broken up, each crofter was allocated a small strip of land on which he built a house. Crofters of the Scottish Highlands are still tenant-farmers of landlords called 'lairds'.

◻ (below) The ancient European system of open fields is shown here in this engraving of the landscape near Cambridge, England. This is before the land was enclosed and the landscape is free of trees or hedges.

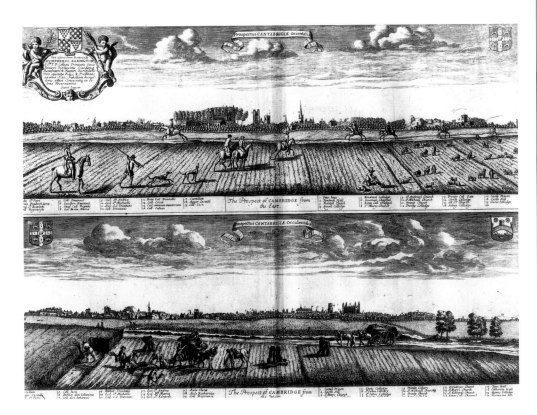

tea, bananas and rubber were introduced, and indigenous people worked as low-wage labourers, or alternatively slave labour was brought in.

Scientific experiments

The 18th century was a time of scientific experimentation in Europe. Enthusiastic landowners soon proved that fertilisers, including manure and lime, could increase yields. They also discovered that land did not have to be left in fallow at all, but by rotating crops that placed different demands on the soil, a crop could be grown in every field all the time.

> Scientific experiments increased the output of farms many-fold and allowed the Industrial Revolution to take place.

The replacement of fallow land with a crop immediately increased the output of farms by a third – enough to provide for the new industrial cities. At the same time experiments with breeding produced animals that would yield more food.

The speed of change

The needs of farmers produced many of the early advances in technology. But the speed of invention dramatically increased in Europe during the 17th and 18th centuries.

It began in 1701 with a machine for sowing seed – Jethro Tull's horse-drawn drill.

Soon a wide variety of tools were being adapted for harvesting the crop. Reapers and threshers could all save enormous amounts of time and help gather the harvest more quickly, preventing spoilage in the fields.

In the days before motor power, the speed that the land could be worked depended on the power of the people and animals that worked the machines. But even gangs of huge shire horses were no match for steam or diesel power.

Plantations past and present

Plantations, or estates, are large farms which today are mainly run by companies. The term has traditionally been used to describe the estates that deal with tropical trees, fibres and foodstuffs, such as cotton, tea, coffee, cocoa and rubber. Many plantations were originally owned by colonial companies and most were staffed with slave labourers. However, even though the colonial powers have gone, and slavery was abolished 150 years ago, the plantation system of farming still thrives.

Plantation crops are generally grown in large fields. The crops are laid out in straight rows in such a way that they can be sprayed, weeded and harvested as much as possible by machine.

All plantation crops are destined to go to food processing companies, and the vast bulk of crops grown in developing countries are sent to markets in industrial countries. In this way the farm products of the developing world earn cash from the industrial world.

❐ (right) Sisal being harvested from a plantation in Tanzania. The hard work involved in harvesting plants is clear from this picture. In the past, slaves would have done this job.

❐ (below) Plantations are still common in the tropics where they occupy large areas of flat fertile land. The fertile slopes of Oahu island, Hawaii (USA), for example, are used for sugar cane and pineapples; the high, cool slopes of Kenya are used for tea plants, and the flat, hot and humid lands of Malaysia for rubber trees.

❏ (below) An 18th century sugar plantation in the West Indies. Slaves are being forced to clear land before a new crop is planted. Such plantations were profitable largely because they did not have to pay wages.

When animal power gave way to machine power, from the late 19th century onwards, the face of farming in the industrial world was greatly changed. But there were even more benefits than a simple increase in power. A fifth of all farmland traditionally had been set aside to provide food for the horses; now it could be used for growing food for people.

The increase in productivity on farms due to enclosures, machines and better sources of power revolutionised the countryside within decades. It also changed the balance between those working on farms and those working in the city for ever. Between the middle of the 18th century and the middle of the 20th century, the proportions of people working on farms dwindled from ninety per cent of the workforce ten per cent, and all without the loss of any output.

Enthusiastic landowners soon proved that fertilisers, including manure and lime, could increase yields.

But this farming revolution was not without its heartache. For those farm labourers in Europe who could not find work in the cities, migration to the United States, Canada, Australia and elsewhere was the only option besides poverty.

Change on the family farm

The family farm that developed in the 17th and 18th centuries became a traditional pattern for 'western' farmers. In many places it still exists today, even though many families face enormous pressures to sell up to big corporations.

The principles on which the family farm works, whether it is on the flat plains of the United States prairies or the rolling hills of southwest England, are just the same. The farm must be of a manageable size, the farmer must choose crops or animal produce that can be taken to market and fetch a good price. It

□ (above) A general farm being worked just before World War II. Horses were still common. Notice the farm buildings in the background and the way the crop is fashioned into 'stooks'. In general, this farm is still geared to a mixture of hand labour and simple machines.

The rise of the General or Mixed Farm

By the turn of this century many farms of industrial world countries had stabilised into family farms. The size of the farm depended on the fertility of the land; in the United States it averaged 65 ha., in Britain about 40 ha., in France and Germany about 20 ha. The distance between farms was often over one km but there was still a great deal of neighbourliness, ready assistance and community life, because all shared the basic need to survive on the farmland.

The family farm was arranged to be self-sufficient, with the family providing much of the labour except, for example, at harvest times when speed was critical. Then they employed teams of labourers who went from farm to farm offering their services, or several farms combined their labour to make a team that could work all the neighbourhood farms.

The main power came from horses, and these, together with a variety of other livestock, were fed from hay gathered on the farm. Dairy cattle were widely kept and milk sold directly off the farm to the local neighbourhood. Poultry would provide eggs and meat; manure from the livestock would be used to return fertiliser to the fields. The normal rotation might be of five or seven years, with cereals, grasses (ley) and perhaps vegetables being grown.

Each farm had a variety of machines, from ploughs and harrows to seed drills and reapers. All were relatively small and scaled to be suited to horse power. Farmers knew how each piece of machinery worked and they could service and, often with the help of a blacksmith, repair it.

Farms had a farmhouse; barns for keeping machines, hay and grains; byres for keeping animals during the winter; and milking parlours, pigsties and poultry houses.

must be able to cope with disasters, so it has to have a variety of products each year just in case bad weather, disease or fluctuations in market prices badly affect any one of them.

Above all a family farm is designed to be handed down from one generation to the next, with the land in just as good condition each time.

All these principles were best brought together in a farm of 40-80 ha., with both crops and animals produced, and with crops and animals being rotated so that the soil in any one field never became impoverished.

The invention of refrigeration and other ways of transporting fresh food changed farming dramatically.

General, or mixed farms were the farmers' natural way to hedge against disaster, because if anything happened to one crop, or the market weakened for one type of animal, the loss could always be balanced against the others. In this way the general farmer is like the self-sufficient farmer. The difference is that the general farm is on a larger scale, and it aims to make a profit, rather than just to survive.

Modern agribusiness

The invention of refrigeration and other ways of preserving food changed farming in a dramatic way. For example, carcasses and dairy products of animals reared in New Zealand, Australia, Argentina and America could be sent to Europe in refrigerated ships; tropical fruits such as bananas could be harvested in Jamaica and sent to North America and Europe to finish ripening. Farmers therefore found themselves faced with overseas competition in a way they had never before experienced. It also meant that the market was important enough for large companies to feel it worthwhile to get involved in farming. Farming and farm products became big business.

Pressures on the family farm

Horses were replaced by steam engines and later by petrol and diesel motors, but essentially the family farm remained unchanged until after World War II.

After the war, larger, more powerful machines were developed that could dramatically cut the time needed for many farm activities.

But such machines are expensive and designed to be used on large farms. They are unsuited to small farms.

So small farms were bought up by larger ones in an effort to keep pace with new technologies. This meant that the number of family farms declined and the number of workers employed fell dramatically.

❑ (above and right) A traditional general farm will have a variety of dairy and beef cattle. Pigs will be fed waste products from the dairying as well as other foods. In this way the farm attempts to be as efficient and balanced as possible.

☐ (above) Although it is a general farm, either cereals or dairy products will be the main source of farm income.

The general farm

General farms, or mixed farms, were developed so that individual farming families could produce a balanced range of products on a farm that was still of manageable size. In contrast to large 'agribusiness' farms, they balance crops and animals, and adopt techniques which do much to conserve the land. Typically a general farm will rotate the use of its fields, and manure from animals kept in stalls will be spread back on to the soil to maintain a well aerated and drained soil structure.

☐ (above right and below) Farm buildings are grouped around the family farmhouse. They include silos for keeping corn dry and haystacks and silage for feeding to animals in winter.

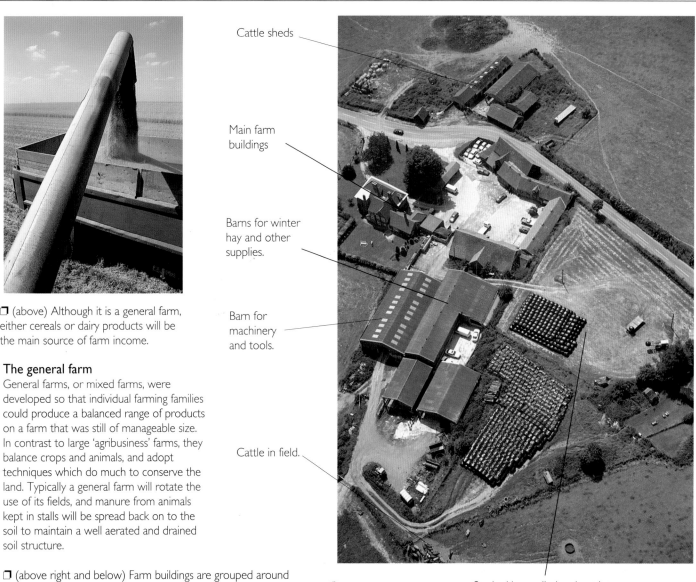

Cattle sheds

Main farm buildings

Barns for winter hay and other supplies.

Barn for machinery and tools.

Cattle in field.

Stacked hay, rolled and put into black plastic bags for fodder.

Larger owners began to buy up smaller farmers. At the same time farmers of the industrial world began to specialise in order to make better use of machines and to reduce the costs of farm labour.

Modern technology also allowed areas to be used in ways that had not been possible before. Traditional irrigation techniques allowed the diversion of rivers, but new powerful pumps could bring water up from water bearing rocks (aquifers) deep below the surface, and modern methods of building dams to store river water allowed irrigation to be practised in vast areas that had never before supported crops. At the same time, research into fertilisers and new seed varieties meant that yields were increased beyond anything that had been thought possible in the past.

> The use of bigger and bigger machines meant that farms needed to be ever-larger to use them efficiently.

The widening gap

At the end of the 19th century, the gap between farmers of the industrial world and the developing world was widening, but not unbridgeable. However, during the 20th century the gap has widened dramatically.

Industrial world countries have become more wealthy and can pay higher prices for their food. This allows farmers to use the newest techniques and machines. In the developing world, many farms are still worked on a small scale, so most people are not able to benefit from new ways of farming.

However, it is a mistake to measure the success of farming in the developing world countries by the number of machines they have or the size of the fields. Developing world countries have large numbers of people who can work their fields by hand and they do not need to replace people with machines.

Collective farms

When the Communist government gained control in the USSR during the 1920s, they planned to overthrow thousands of years of farming tradition. They took land away from individual farmers and put it under state control. The huge state-run farms, were known as collective farms. This was a dramatic change, affecting hundreds of millions of people and was introduced with very little understanding of the long-term results.

Every state farm was made part of a giant plan for feeding the entire country at fixed low prices. Each collective farm had to meet certain production targets each year, and prices were set by the government. Each farm employed thousands of workers.

The reorganisation of farming on such a giant scale caused great upheaval. Entire regions found themselves growing the same crop, because each region was planned to supply the needs of the whole country. At the same time they had to import all their other food needs from distant regions.

In China, collective farms were introduced in 1949. They were known as communes, each based on groups of villages and tens of thousands of people.

❏ (below) China's communes make use of large numbers of people using very simple tools. Large machines are rare and most cultivating, and even transport, is done by people.

Although most tasks are done by hand, there are some small powered machines. They can be adapted to a wide range of tasks such as 'puddling' the paddy, threshing and pumping water.

These people are harvesting using sickles.

Farming on Chinese communes varies greatly over the country depending on the climate. In the favoured south three crops can be grown; in the north cold winters prevent more than one crop a year.

Produce is mostly transported on foot and by bicycle.

❐ (right) A commune is harvesting rice from the paddy fields.

A scheme that went disastrously wrong

Collective farming is based on political ideas, not on the needs of the land. Decisions were not made by farmers who knew best what would grow on their land, but by officials in distant cities. Farm workers had no reason to work hard because once they reached their production targets they would be paid no more, no matter how much effort they put in.

Strict collective ideas caused farm output to drop and both the USSR and China were often forced to import grain to feed their people, something they had never before had to do. People in the countryside are now given private plots to grow vegetables and sell them on the open market. They can even sell any surplus. This has made life much easier.

❐ (below) A commune village in China.

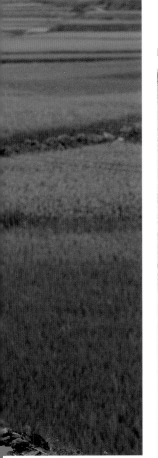

The most important step to getting more from the land has been the introduction of better seeds and better ways of farming. For example, many new seed varieties have been produced, some of which have allowed farmers to more than double, and in some cases more than treble, their yield.

The Green Revolution was important in giving new strains of crops, but it also made farmers take a fresh look at their own local varieties.

The introduction of some of these new varieties, especially of rice and wheat, has been called the Green Revolution. By sharing ideas and the enthusiasm for improvement, many countries in the developing world are getting a surplus.

A time of surplus

The Green Revolution has helped many countries of the developing world prevent starvation. The same new seeds used in the industrial world have given such huge yields that now there is great over-supply and surplus.

Most industrial world governments have been forced to pile up surpluses while looking for ways of actually reducing farm yields. They cannot sell the surpluses on the world market at low cost because cheap food would simply put the developing world's farmers out of business.

So as this century comes to a close the world's farming is still causing problems worldwide. The successes of farming have meant that, while the developing world is just managing to get by, and there are still major areas with real food shortages, other areas have surpluses they cannot even give away. Indeed, the industrial world's farmers are so productive that governments are looking for ways of taking land out of production.

The Green Revolution

One of the world's major problems is to produce enough food for the developing world. The Green Revolution is a term used to refer to a wide range of improvements in developing world farming, including better seed and training for farmers in growing their crops more effectively.

Several international research organisations were set up to develop high yielding varieties (HYV) of crops. The first was The International Maize and Wheat Improvement Centre, based in Mexico. Another research centre was the International Rice Research Institute in the Philippines.

By the 1960s they had succeeded in improving both wheat and rice seed (although maize is harder to improve). One of the most spectacular varieties of rice (code-named IR8) gave such high yields that it was called 'the miracle rice'.

Improved wheat and rice seeds have since been widely used in countries such as India and Malaysia. When used with fertilisers, the increase in yield has been dramatic.

In the long run, perhaps the most important strength of the Green Revolution was that it got farmers to take a fresh look at their own local varieties, and to experiment with how they could increase the yields of the more traditional crops.

Why the Green Revolution can fail

The Green Revolution might seem like the way forward for the developing world, but this is not entirely true. High yielding varieties are less resistant to drought and more prone to pests and diseases. For a good yield of wheat, for example, irrigation has to be used to make sure that enough moisture is available through the growing season.

In places such as the area called the Sahel, just south of the Sahara desert in Africa, there are no major rivers to be tapped for irrigation water. As a result, it has been much more difficult to get success with new varieties and the people are better off using traditional crops, even if the yield is low. So while Asian countries may have benefited, African countries have largely missed out on the Green Revolution simply because their climate and landscape are not favourable.

❒ (left) The Green Revolution has also benefited the industrial countries because newer varieties of crops can be used wherever the climate is suitable.

❒ (below) One of the key reasons for success has been the development of small, cheap machines that are suited to paddy fields.

❒ (below) Advances in pesticides and new strains of crops have increased yields considerably, but often at a high cost to the environment.

□ (above) To be adequately fed each of us needs the equivalent of 250 kg of grain each year.

Understanding the food we need

Countries of the developing world trying to feed their people need to know how much value there is in every kind of food. In this way they can know how to ensure everyone has a balanced, healthy diet.

Different foods contain different amounts of energy. For example 1 g of pure protein will yield 4 calories, 1 g of pure fat will yield 9 calories, and 1 g of pure carbohydrate (sugars and starches) will yield 4 calories.

People need energy to power their bodies. Fats (mostly obtained from animals) are the most concentrated energy source, but also the most expensive; carbohydrates are the cheapest source of energy. Grains (e.g. rice), pulses (e.g. beans), tubers (e.g. potatoes), and roots (e.g. cassava) provide starch. Sugars occur in many fruits, which are also a good source of vitamins.

Many people suffer from lack of protein, which causes problems with growth and makes people less resistant to disease. As a result they have a shorter life span.

Eating a variety of plants will be just as good as eating the protein-rich meat from animals. It is simply a matter of eating more.

Drinks can provide as much nourishment as solid foods. For example, whole milk contains 5% carbohydrate, 3.5% fat, 3.5% protein (as well as 88% water).

What can be done to feed the world?

The world produces more than enough food to feed everyone, yet 500 million people do not get enough to eat. The reason for MALNUTRITION and famine is simply that *people cannot afford to buy the food that exists.*

This can only be solved if people can find jobs to earn the money to buy what food there is. It is a question of politics more than environment or farmland.

In India, for example, output from the farms has risen by nearly three per cent a year, nearly one per cent more than the rate of increase of its people. Thus, by 1985 India had three million tonnes of food grains that its people could not afford to buy, and over fourteen months' of stocks for emergencies. Yet half the population still cannot afford to have two square meals a day, even with state subsidised ration shops.

Feeding the world will not get any simpler until people in general can be made more prosperous.

□ (right) This picture shows how rows of trees and crops can be grown together.

Developing from traditional systems

Some farming communities, especially in Africa, have found life increasingly difficult. Many traditional ways of farming cannot support large numbers of people. The land becomes over-used and yields go down. But there are ways they can be helped.

For example, most people in the developing world use land as a source of wood (for fuel) as well as food. As they overwork the land they also destroy the trees they depend on. Feeding the world is therefore a matter of getting better yields and leaving some land to grow wood.

A lot can be gained, for example, by mixing trees and crops. Some trees can help increase yields dramatically and at the same time can be cropped for firewood and stakes. Some of its leaves can also be taken for fodder in the dry season.

This system uses many plants that are familiar to the farmers, and because they are native plants, they are also hardy. It is quite easy to show farmers the advantage of the system, because it provides improvements within a few years. This means that farmers can increase their yield and obtain a yield from the tree as a bonus.

□ (right) The best way to help farmers is to find ways of adapting their farming to give better yields.

❐ (below) Arms outstretched as he explains the problems of producing more food from a reluctant land, this African farmer expresses the feelings of farmers across the world. As populations grow and people seek lower prices for their food, more and more pressure is placed on farmland and farmers, while farmers are given less and less sympathy.

Farmers worldwide must preserve the land for future generations. But more and more people means less and less land for each farmer, forcing many to farm in ways which go against their better judgment, but which still give a yield in the short term. African farmers are not alone in being under pressure.

Chapter 3

World crops

The world's people depend on crops as the mainstay of their diets. The great variety of crops that have been developed is the result of people selecting from many natural species.

What is grown in any one place depends on climate and soil, how much money can be invested in growing the crop and the personal taste of the farmers and their customers.

Farmers are always faced with the question: 'How can I make the most from my land?' They begin by looking at the two different alternatives: growing crops or rearing animals.

For people who are trying to survive it is far more efficient to grow crops than to rear animals, providing the soil and climate will allow it. This is why the majority of the world's small farmers are cultivators rather than pastoralists. Even in the countries where farming is done on a large scale and farmers work for profit, the majority will still grow crops, even if they then feed them to animals.

Selecting what to grow

By carefully choosing the crops they will grow, farmers can make the best use of their climate and soils. For example, if grains give unreliable yields because summers tend to be wet, farmers will then choose to grow vegetables. On the other hand dry conditions may favour cereals over vegetables.

The price the market will pay for each crop will influence how much investment a farmer will make. For example market garden produce

☐ (left) Planting rice in Bali (Indonesia).

commands relatively high prices, making it profitable for farmers in cool climates to spend money on growing produce in greenhouses or in cloches (tunnels of plastic). Similarly, a suitably high price will encourage farmers in hot, dry regions to invest in irrigation, either by diverting water from rivers or pumping it from underground.

The choice of crops may also be influenced by the need to insure against harvest failure. Farmers will grow more than one crop if the chances of failure are high, so that if one crop fails, others will still provide an income for the year.

The advantages of cereals

Growing cereals lends itself to farming on every scale, from plots of no more than a few tens of square metres to those covering hundreds of square kilometres. Grain, with its nutritional value (see below and page 7) is a staple part of the diet in many regions of the world. Grain farming is therefore the main task of most of the world's farmers.

> **Grain, the seed of cereal plants, is the most widespread product of arable-land crops, and one of the most basic foodstuffs.**

Wild grasses (the ancestors of modern cereal plants) are among the most widely distributed of all plant families, growing from the hot tropics to the cold tundra. This is why you may see farmers successfully coaxing grains to ripen in the Arctic as well as in the tropics. Each cereal variety is best suited to a particular range of climates and moisture conditions, which is why the major grains – rice, wheat, maize, barley, oats, rye, sorghum and millet – are not usually all found growing together.

Grains have many advantages. They are the least expensive way of providing people with energy and with many of the vitamins, minerals and proteins needed for healthy living.

Rice cultivation

Wild rice grows in places that have warm summers and where the soil is marshy or waterlogged for much of the year. Some cultivated varieties of rice (known as 'dry' rice, because they can grow without waterlogging) can simply be planted during the wet season. However, the yield is higher and more reliable from those rice varieties that are planted in paddy fields (fields surrounded by mud walls that can be flooded by irrigation water). Flooded fields also helps to keep weeds under control. By irrigating paddy fields during the dry season, two and sometimes three rice crops can be grown on the same fields each year.

In most parts of the world large numbers of farm workers are used to plough the land and to plant, weed and harvest the rice. Rice seedlings are spaced out by hand into the soft muddy soils of the flooded fields. The fields are then kept flooded until just before harvesting, when they are drained.

The rice plant
Rice is derived from a wide variety of swamp grasses. Cultivated rice grows up to 1 m high. The roots are adapted to extract oxygen as well as nourishment from waterlogged soil.

Each variety of rice displayed in these sacks is used for different cooking purposes: the display includes long-grained rice, short-grained rice, sticky rice, and so on.

The paddy rice-growing cycle

1 (above) In the wet season water is channelled from rivers into the fields. Rice is planted by hand by people standing ankle deep in the muddy fields.

2 (above) The rice grows quickly in moist, warm conditions and as it matures the fields take on a rich, emerald green appearance. During this period the fields have to be weeded; sometimes fertiliser and pesticides are also sprayed onto the plants.

A rice grain has a brown coating – a hull and a bran coat – that contains most of the vitamins. White rice is the kernel only. It is not as healthy as brown (unmilled) rice, but the hull is difficult to eat.

Rice (including hull) contains 10% protein, 65% starch, 5% vitamins and minerals.

White rice is often coated with a vitamin and mineral supplement before being sold. The hulls are used to feed animals.

Grain is harvested from about 150 million ha. of paddy worldwide each year, giving a yield of 350–400 million tonnes.

The main use of rice is as food. In most eastern countries it is the staple grain, eaten with every meal. In the west it is mainly processed and used for breakfast cereals and baby foods.

There are more than 7000 different rice varieties. This gives plenty of opportunity to grow rice for different purposes.

Rice can be refined to make an edible oil and distilled to make alcoholic drinks, such as Japanese *sake* and Chinese rice wine. Laundry starch is made from rice.

3 (above) When the rice has ripened, the fields are drained and the rice harvested. Traditionally, small fields are harvested by hand using knives or sickles. Where labour is in short supply, such as in the Philippines and Thailand, small harvesting machines (powered by motorbike motors) are used. In places with large fields or expensive labour, the rice is harvested like wheat, with giant combine harvesters.

After harvest the fields are left dry and brown until it is time to flood them again.

Grains can be stored easily once they have been harvested. Provided they are kept dry and protected from great heat, grains will not rot or deteriorate. This is why they were grown by farmers from the earliest times and why they remain the most important farming product.

Rice

More people eat rice than any other of the world's grains. Rice was first cultivated in China, Japan, India and Southeast Asia. It was introduced to Africa and the Middle East over two thousand years ago. It was first planted in North America in 1685 and found to grow well in the states of Mississippi and Texas. Later it was also grown in California.

> When it is carefully tended, the yields from rice are higher than any other cereal crop except for maize.

Thailand, China, India, Indonesia, Bangladesh and Japan are the leading rice-growing countries. Most is produced for home consumption. Only three per cent of the rice grown in the world is exported, mostly by industrial world countries such as the United States and Australia. The United States, for example, produces about five million tonnes of rice each year, nearly half of which is exported, often as food aid.

Wheat

Wheat was first grown in the Middle East over 9000 years ago. Since then several different varieties have been produced: hard wheat, used for bread; durum wheat, used for pasta, such as spaghetti; and soft wheat used for cakes and pastries.

The kernel (inside) is surrounded by a hull which is difficult to remove and makes up 15% of the grain. Flour must therefore be ground, or milled, to separate the hull from the kernel.

Wheat cultivation

Wheat is planted on a seed bed that has been prepared by ploughing and harrowing. Many farmers plant the seeds in the autumn and growth begins before the winter. These 'winter wheat' plants then grow swiftly at the start of spring.

New forms of wheat have short stems and do not easily fall over during rainstorms. Most of the world's wheat is harvested with combine harvesting machines.

Over 400 million tonnes of wheat are grown each year on 240 million ha. of arable land. The main wheat producers are the former USSR, the United States, China, India, Canada, France, Turkey and Australia. Major wheat-exporting countries are the United States, Canada, Australia and Argentina.

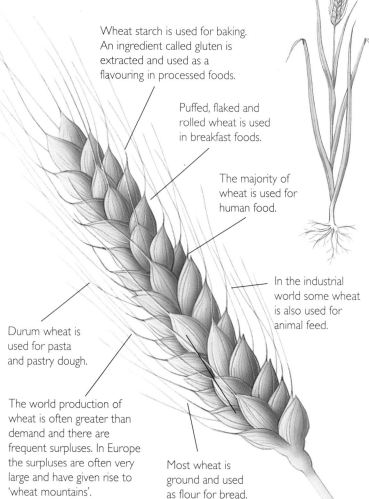

The wheat plant
Wheat is a grass with a hollow bluish-green stem that will ripen to a yellow colour even in cool climates. Its seed head contains up to a hundred seeds, surrounded with short hairs. Modern wheat has a stout stem, bred to improve resistance to storm damage. It is rarely taller than about 60 cm.

Wheat starch is used for baking. An ingredient called gluten is extracted and used as a flavouring in processed foods.

Puffed, flaked and rolled wheat is used in breakfast foods.

The majority of wheat is used for human food.

In the industrial world some wheat is also used for animal feed.

Durum wheat is used for pasta and pastry dough.

The world production of wheat is often greater than demand and there are frequent surpluses. In Europe the surpluses are often very large and have given rise to 'wheat mountains'.

Most wheat is ground and used as flour for bread.

□ (below) Wheat and maize sometimes have to be harvested in damp conditions. To reduce the moisture content to levels that will allow it to be stored and transported, farmers store grain in tall silos containing huge hot air blowers.

□ (above) In countries like the United States, scientific research means the yield of corn increases by an about 160 kg/ha. each year. At the same time machines improve productivity as well. Fifty years ago each 25 kg of corn took thirty minutes of labour to produce; now it takes less than three minutes.

Maize cultivation

In developed countries, maize cultivation is done entirely by machine. As the plants grow they are sprayed, to keep away pests and diseases, and fed with fertilisers.

Varieties of corn have been developed which grow to uniform heights and ripen at the same time. This allows the ripe plants to be harvested by machines. The machines pick the cobs and shell them at the same time. Finally, the field is cleared with machines that can cut up the stalks and leaves to make silage for cattle feed.

Over 130 million ha. of land are planted with maize, giving more than 440 million tonnes of grain each year. The major producers are the United States (which produces forty per cent of the world total), China, Brazil, the former USSR, Mexico, Argentina, Romania, France, India, and South Africa.

The maize (corn) plant
Maize is the tallest cereal plant and can reach up to 4 m. The jointed cornstalk (stem) looks like thin bamboo.

Each plant can carry three or more large cobs (seed heads) each with rows of pale yellow seeds.

Cobs grow from the stem joints. Each cob is cloaked by green leaves and a tassel of fibres.

Corn extracts can be used as a thickener in the food processing industries.

Less than two per cent of corn is used for human food in the industrial world; in the developing world it is almost all used for food.

Corn can be used in making spirits and fuel.

Corn syrup is used as a sugar substitute in some foods.

Nearly half of all corn grown in the United States is used to fatten cattle, pigs and poultry.

In developing countries corn is ground down to make maize meal and boiled to soften the grain. It is eaten as a kind of porridge or baked to make a flat bread.

Wheat grows best in warm to cool, fairly dry climates. In Europe it has been grown for many centuries on the plains of central Spain, northern France and eastern England. The Spanish took it to the Americas in 1519, and the British introduced it to Australia in the 19th century. It is now grown all over the world.

Maize

Maize, or corn, is the tallest of the grain plants, reaching over 4 m, with a jointed stem from which the cobs grow. It is a native of Central America and was used as a food by Mexicans more than 7000 years ago.

Maize does not tolerate damp and cool conditions or poor soils. It thrives best where the soil is deep, fertile, well drained and warm, and where the climate is hot throughout the growing season. One of the most suitable areas is the part of the United States prairies south of Chicago known as the Corn Belt.

Vegetables

Vegetables are herbaceous plants that are grown for their leaves (e.g. cabbage), roots (e.g. carrot, beetroot), stems (e.g. asparagus), tubers (e.g. potato), bulbs (e.g. onion), flowers (e.g. broccoli), seeds (e.g. beans), fruit (e.g. marrow, cucumber), and leaf stalks (e.g. rhubarb). Potatoes, cabbage, tomatoes, lettuce and onions are the most commercially important vegetables.

> Vegetables yield a much greater value per hectare than cereal crops.

Vegetable are an extremely important crop because they can be grown on every scale, from tiny garden plots to huge fields. They will tolerate a wide range of climates and provide a reliable harvest.

Vegetables do not take a lot of nourishment from the soil in the same way as cereals, so they will grow on poor soil and they do not have to be given large amounts of fertiliser.

Producing field vegetables

Vegetables yield a much greater value per hectare than cereal crops. This means that farmers with suitable soil can use many people, and apply fertilisers, and water during a drought. This is known as intensive cultivation.

There are great variations between the way that vegetables grow and are harvested. Tubers and bulbs, such as potatoes, carrots and onions, do not easily rot, nor are they easily damaged by machine. They can therefore be harvested mechanically.

On the other hand, many other types of vegetable are at their peak of freshness and quality for only a few days. Some, like lettuce, are also easily bruised and need to be handled carefully. Many fruit and leaf vegetables therefore have to be harvested by hand.

Vegetables that are not intended for shops, but that are meant for the food processing industry, do not have to be handled so carefully and are nearly all picked by machine. Frozen peas and canned tomatoes are two common examples.

❏ (above) A field of swedes.

Potato

Potatoes are tubers that grow from underground stems. The plants are stocky, with deep green leaves. They grow in cool, moist climates to reach less than 1 m high.

Potatoes are very important to many human diets. A diet of just potatoes and milk would, for example, give all the nourishment that a body needs.

Potatoes rank, after wheat, rice, and maize, as the world's fourth most important crop by weight. The former USSR, Poland, and the United States grow most potatoes.

Potato tubers are planted in the soil in rows. As the plant grows, the growing tubers are covered with soil. This process, called 'earthing up' covers the potato field with long ridges and furrows during the growing season.

Soybean

The soybean produces an edible oil and a high protein food that can be used as a meat substitute and to make margarine. It is also grown as fodder for animals.

The soybean does not grow naturally in the wild but was first cultivated in China, thousands of years ago. Now two thirds of world production is in the United States.

❐ (above) Vegetables are a popular crop in the developing world because intensive cultivation gives high yields, and labour costs are low. These cucumbers are being grown on the bed of a river during the dry season in India. The farmer is using the natural fertility and moisture of the river bed. He has to hope that his crop will mature before the rainy season arrives and washes it away.

❐ (below and right) Greenhouse growing of vegetables is important in some areas, and significant quantities of tomatoes, cucumbers and lettuce are grown in forcing structures. Mushroom production is a specialised part of the vegetable industry.

Pipes take water directly to roots of crop.

Sprinkler system regulates humidity.

The vegetables grown in greenhouses are often unsuitable for growing outside.

They are also a rich source of vitamins and minerals and supply fibre bulk. Vegetables are also low in calories, making them attractive in industrial world countries where people tend to be overweight; but they need a calorie-rich supplement, such as rice, in developing world countries where malnutrition can be a problem.

Most vegetables are treated as annuals, and their seeds planted each year. Commercial growers prefer sandy loam soils, which are light enough to fall away easily from the plants when they are harvested. It is rare to find vegetables being grown in a heavy clay soil.

> Vegetables are an extremely important crop because they can be grown on every scale, from tiny garden plots to huge fields.

In the past vegetable farming was found near all large cities. However, now that faster transport and refrigerated trucks are available, and especially since the invention of freezing techniques, vegetable farming tends to be concentrated where soils and climate are best. For example, about half of all commercial vegetables in the United States are grown in California, and the majority of vegetables in the United Kingdom are grown in the East Anglian fens.

Fruits

For farming purposes, fruits are found on perennial bushes or trees. The fruits of annual plants (such as the tomato and soybean) are grouped with vegetables.

Fruits are important farm crops, and they are grown in both temperate and tropical lands. Typical temperate fruits include apples, pears, grapes and strawberries. Warm temperate fruits include all the citrus fruits (such as oranges and lemons), and figs and olives, while tropical fruits include bananas and pineapples.

'Tree' fruits

People eat tree fruits because they taste nice, but also because they contain a range of vitamins that are important to good health.

Apples, peaches, pears, plums and cherries are the most important tree fruits of cool climates. Important fruit crops of warm climates include lemons, limes, oranges and apricots. Dates and figs are important in near-desert regions; olives and tangerines are small trees of the Mediterranean climates. Fruits of tropical climates include bananas (not a true tree), mangos (the fruit of a giant tropical tree), and pawpaws (papaya) which grow on a tropical tree with a single straight stem.

❐ (below) Bananas are actually large herbs, but they look like trees. They grow up to 10 m in height. This picture shows the flowering stalk and behind it the cluster of seeds in their fleshy cases: the bananas.

☐ (above) An orchard commonly has hundreds or thousands of trees spaced in straight lines. The trees are cut back – pruned – to encourage more fruiting growth and a tree of suitable shape and size for easy harvesting.

Apple

No tree is more widely cultivated than the apple, and its fruit is second only to the orange in worldwide production. Many types of apple are grown for their juice, as cooking apples or as eating (dessert) apples.

Orchards (plantations of apple trees) contain trees which may be cultivated in many ways, from dwarf trees to full-sized trees. They may be trained along wires for ease of picking.

Apples grow best where the climate is cool. Some apples grown in warmer regions of, for example, southern France, grow too quickly and do not develop as rich a flavour as those grown farther north.

Western Europe produces more apples than any other region, but Argentina, Chile, and Japan have large orchards. In the United States, too, the northern (cooler) states produce apples.

☐ (above) Fruit irrigation.

Citrus fruits

Citrus fruits are grown on evergreen trees and shrubs that originated in Southeast Asia. They are now grown worldwide in tropical and subtropical regions, especially in North and South America, the Mediterranean region, Australia, and South Africa. The most important citrus fruit is the orange, which comprises two-thirds of world citrus production. Other citrus fruits include the tangerine, lemon, lime and grapefruit

Citrus fruits need water to grow their soft fleshy fruits, and many citrus plantations make great use of irrigation.

Temperature has an important effect on the quality of the fruit. Thus, while apples will grow well in warm temperate and even subtropical conditions, the warm conditions produce a less intense flavour than apples that grow in cooler regions, where they mature more slowly.

Similarly, warm temperate fruits, such as the citrus fruits and grapes, will not have a sufficiently long warm period to ripen if they are grown in cooler climates.

A fruit's flavour can be affected by the climate as well as by the soil. Grapes grown in neighbouring fields but on different soils can taste completely different.

In the cool temperate regions, the main control on successful farming is the length of cold conditions during winter. If the winter is mild, and cold conditions (known as chilling) do not occur often enough, the fruit trees may not blossom or set seed.

Fruits are particularly difficult to store, although apples and some other fruits can be stored for months at controlled low temperatures. In general, because ripening cannot be stopped, fruits that have to reach markets a long way away are harvested before they are fully ripe. Thus bananas are always harvested when green, although when they arrive at their markets they will have ripened and turned yellow.

Tropical fruit

Over half the commercially cultivated tropical fruits have their origins in the Americas, although almost all are now found worldwide. The number of tropical fruits grown for commercial reasons is far smaller than the numbers eaten locally, in part because some fruits have an acquired taste, and also because not all have been successfully cultivated.

Bush and vine

A wide range of edible products come from bushes and vines around the world. The most common are the coffee and tea bushes and the grape vine.

Coffee

Almost everyone throughout the world drinks coffee, and the coffee bean is worth more than any other farm crop, including all the cereals! Two types of coffee, Coffea arabica and Coffea robusta, make up 99 percent of the total world output.

Coffee plants are evergreen shrubs that grow about 1.5–2 m high. They need a hot, moist climate and do not tolerate frost. The best beans grow on the flanks of mountains at between 1000 and 2000 m above sea level.

A coffee tree takes five years to produce fruit and then each plant will yield 2 kg of red, seed-bearing coffee 'cherries'. From this, about 0.5 kg of green coffee beans are obtained. The cherries must be picked by hand to make sure that only red, ripe berries are selected.

South America and Africa produce most of the world's coffee, but because it is potentially such a profitable crop, many other countries, such as Indonesia and Papua New Guinea have also become coffee producers.

Tea

Tea is a small evergreen bush. Its leaves, when dried can be made into a drink.

Most tea is grown on plantations, sometimes called gardens or estates. Tea will only grow in rich soils where the air is humid. The best tea plants are grown at between 1000 and 2000 m where the slow growth allows the leaves to develop a richer flavour.

India (by far the largest), Sri Lanka, China, Japan, Indonesia, Kenya, Georgia, Azerbaijan and Australia are among the world's leading producers of tea.

❐ (right) Tea bushes in Queensland (Australia).

❐ (below) Tea leaves being collected in Kenya.

Grapes

Grapes are berries of a range of plants that grow as vines. Grapes with about a fifth of their content as sugar are used to make wine. All other types are used for eating fresh or for drying to make raisins.

About 10 million ha. of grapes are cultivated worldwide. Italy, Spain, France, the former USSR and Turkey have the largest areas of vineyards.

Wine is made from fermented grape juice. Although it covers a tiny part of the world's farmland, growing grapes for wine is one of the world's most important farming activities.

The crop is harvested in the autumn when the grapes contain the optimum balance of sugar and acidity. For the sweet white wines of Bordeaux and Germany, picking is delayed until the grapes are affected by a beneficial mould, which concentrates the juice by dehydration.

The juice of most grape varieties is colourless. For red wine, the grapes are crushed immediately after picking and the stems are generally removed.

❐ (above) A Californian winery surrounded by grapes growing on vines.

❐ (below) In France, tradition is still important, and many of the vineyards are organised so that crops can be picked by hand. Few machines are seen in the fields.

Traditionally the grapes were picked and then processed by people of small villages like the one shown here.

❐ (above left) Grapes growing in a French vineyard.

Industrial crops

Farmers grow a wide variety of crops for their fibres, sap and oil. These are classified as industrial crops because they are not eaten. They include cotton, flax and jute. Jute and flax plants are harvested and the fibre extracted from the stems; cotton surrounds the seeds to make a cotton 'boll'.

Cotton is the most important industrial crop. Farmers produce about twenty million tonnes of raw cotton each year.

Cotton requires a hot rainy climate for its growth. The largest producers are China (which produces a quarter of the world's cotton), the former USSR, the United States, India and Pakistan. Brazil, Turkey and Egypt produce lesser amounts.

❐ (above) Cotton is grown as an annual plant. The cotton fibres (called lint) grow from the surface cells of the cotton seeds until they form a seed head packed with lint. This is known as a cotton boll. Each of the fibres is about 2 cm long.

Growing industrial crops

Some of the most widely harvested fruits and seeds are used for making vegetable oils. The most important annual crops are soybeans, oil-seed rape, sunflower and palm. Soybeans are favoured in North America and oil-seed rape has gained great favour in European countries, where it is being grown as a substitute for imported tropical vegetable oils.

Rubber

Natural rubber is a watery white liquid called latex that oozes from just below the bark of a range of tropical trees. The bark is cut, or tapped, with a knife, making diagonal scars across the tree. The latex that drips from the scars is collected in a small cup.

The rubber tree, a native of South America, was transported to many British colonies in Asia during the middle of the 19th century. It is now grown in hundreds of thousands of smallholder woods and also on some large plantations, where it is cultivated just like field crops. Asia now produces ninety per cent of the world's supply; Malaysia alone provides half of the world total.

❐ (above) Tapping the rubber tree.

Oil seeds

There area variety of seeds that can be used to produce oils. Sunflower, rape and linseed are the most common crops grown in the fields. These annual plants produce brightly coloured flowers; the rape is mustard yellow, the linseed is a pale blue.

The seed is found in pods which are crushed until the soil can be extracted.

Palms

The palm family comprises nearly 2500 species that occur throughout the tropics and subtropics. Palm fruit like the coconut, for example, is biologically like a peach except that the husk is made of fibre instead of a juicy flesh. In Asia the commonest palm product in use is the fruit of the betel-nut palm, which is chewed.

The most important African palm is the date palm, The most important Asian palms are used for oils.

Sugar

Sugar comes mainly from a tropical cane and from a cool-climate beet. Sugar cane farming began in the 16th century on early slave plantations. About sixty per cent of the sugar produced comes from cane.

Sugar beet was discovered in the 18th century. It gave people in Europe and North America a way of making sugar without importing it from overseas. About forty per cent of world production of sugar is from beets.

Sugar cane can grow to over 4 m high. The sugar in cane sugar is contained in the stalks of the grass-like plant. It is processed in a sugar mill to extract the cane juice.

Sugar beets grow in fields and look like like swedes or turnips. They are heavy and bulky and the refinery is always situated in the area where the beets are grown. The remains of sugar beet plants are fed to animals as fodder.

❐ (below) A palm oil plantation in Malaysia. The nuts are collected and taken to a processing plant where they are crushed, heated and the oil extracted.

❐ (below) A sugar cane factory processes the stalks of the sugar cane grass (left).

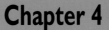
The world's farm animals

Animals are often thought of as just a source of food. However, animals can also be used as a source of power, such as for pulling ploughs; they can yield fibres such as wool which can be made into clothes; and their hides and skins can be used for shoes and clothes. Even their bones can be used for fertiliser (bone meal) and glue, and their dung can be used for cooking and heating fuel.

Only a quarter of the Earth's surface is suitable for growing crops; far more is suitable for grazing (from grasses) or browsing (from shrubs). Even in areas where plants can be cultivated successfully for their seeds, fruits or roots, animals can make far more use of the plant remains than humans ever could.

People began to domesticate suitable wild animals over 10,000 years ago. Pastoral farming, called animal husbandry, allows more people to live in a much wider range of environments than if they had to rely on crops alone.

Animals can help people to make more use of the land, but only if they do not compete for the same food. This is why people in developing world countries feed plant remains to animals. In the developing world about a quarter of the protein people eat comes from animal products.

Industrialised countries, whose croplands provide far more than their needs, have

☐ (left) Beef being reared on poor Highland grazing in Scotland before being transferred to lowlands for the last stages of fattening. They are known as 'store' cattle.

increasingly fed cereals to animals. This is a fast way of fattening the animals, but an inefficient, and therefore expensive, way of providing people with food. Thus, although only about a third of all protein eaten by humans worldwide comes from animals, in prosperous regions, such as North America, Western Europe and Australia, animal protein makes up about three quarters of the average human diet.

Many uses for animals

Not all wild animals have proved to be easy to domesticate, which is the reason so few species are used as farm animals. The main domesticated farm animals are pigs, chickens, ducks, turkeys, goats, sheep, cattle, horses, donkeys, camels, rabbits and reindeer. Most of the domesticated animals originated in Asia and have subsequently been introduced worldwide; there were fewer species in America and Australia that could be domesticated.

> Farming with animals allows people to live in a much wider range of environments than if they had to rely on crops alone.

Breeding has changed the uses as well as the looks of most farm animals. For example, wild cattle only produce the small amounts of milk needed for their calves whereas modern dairy cattle produce many litres of milk each day. Chickens now lay eggs daily in contrast to wildfowl that lay eggs only once a year.

❐ (above) A water hole on the ranges of the Great Plains (USA).

Where beef cattle are reared

India is the largest cattle-raising country, but its cattle are not for beef because they are regarded as sacred animals. In India cattle must not be slaughtered, although their milk is widely drunk and they are used to pull carts.

In other countries cattle are used both for milk and meat. Brazil is the world's second largest cattle rearing country, much of it on land that has been produced by clearing tropical rainforest. The former USSR, the United States, China, Australia and Argentina make up the other major producers of cattle. In these countries, as elsewhere, the main use of cattle is for beef, with only about a tenth of the total cattle numbers used for milk production.

Beef consumption is higher in the United States than anywhere else in the world. Beef has to be imported from Australia and Argentina to match the demand.

Specialising in beef farming

Beef farming is concerned with raising cattle to put on as much weight as possible in the shortest practicable time and at the lowest cost. Rearing beef cattle takes about two years, with the animals adding weight on average by about 1 kg a day.

Three separate farmers may be involved in rearing a beef cow The first stage may involve a dairy farmer, who calves his cows regularly so that they remain in milk. For about six months the calves are allowed to stay with their mothers, consuming natural milk.

Then they are sold to a farmer who allows them to grow up.

Finally, when the calves are perhaps a year to eighteen months, they are sold again through the market, this time to a lowland farmer who will rear the animals for slaughter through a programme of fast fattening.

Many beef cattle are crossbreeds, produced as calves from dairy cattle as part of the programme of keeping the cows in milk.

□ (right) Some cattle – oxen and water buffalo – are also valued as draught, or power, animals. In some countries cattle are a measure of the wealth and status of farmers in their communities.

□ (above) Feedlots where cattle are fattened using corn. This is a fast way of getting cattle to put on weight, but if it were eaten directly it would feed nine times as many people as can be fed on the slaughtered animals.

2 As soon as they are old enough to be independent, the calves are sold to a farmer who owns grazing land of average to poor quality. This may be dry rangeland or upland pasture. Here the animals are allowed to grow up. At this stage, as store cattle, the quality of the grazing is less important.

3 Finally the cattle are fattened on lowland farms or in feedlots before being sent for slaughter.

Cattle

Cattle are the largest domesticated animals. A fully grown bull can weigh well over a tonne; a dairy cow may weigh over half a tonne. People have found cattle particularly useful farm animals because they can provide over three hundred products, including milk, meat, leather and dung.

> Cattle are particularly useful farm animals because they can provide over 300 products.

There are two main varieties of cattle; those found in temperate countries, such as the Hereford, Friesian and Guernsey breeds, and those more suited to tropical regions such as the Zebu with its distinctive flaps of skin.

Selective breeding

Cattle were traditionally thought of as all-purpose animals. The cattle taken by Columbus to America were of this type and they proved well adapted to the dry, hot summers. The Texas Longhorn, perhaps America's most famous beef cattle, was descended from the all-purpose animal.

❏ (above) In both Asia and Europe farmers had a wide variety of wild animals that could be domesticated. Sheep and goats were the first domesticated animals. They were grazed on the grasslands that were unsuited to cropping. In America there were fewer suitable animals, most of those used today are descended from European and Asian breeds. This picture shows a new breed of cattle being judged in 1837.

World milk production

Dairy cattle thrive best in temperate regions, and here about 85% of the total world milk is produced. People in East and Southeast Asia use very little milk because it is not to their taste.

India has by far the largest number of cattle. Most are kept for religious purposes and almost none are slaughtered for beef; instead they are milked. However, with limited amounts of concentrates and restricted breeding, India's total production per head of cattle is low.

The largest milk producer is the former USSR, followed by the United States (dominated by the cool north-central states), France and the United Kingdom. In countries such as New Zealand, dairy produce, in the form of butter and cheese in particular, is a major export earner.

Dairy cattle would not normally produce high yields in dry lands because they could not get enough energy from the pastures. So in areas where there is high demand for dairy products but where natural pastures are rare (such as California, USA), dairy cattle are kept in pens or feedlots where they are fed hay and concentrates brought in from other parts of the country.

In most industrial countries, farmers have been able to increase the milk from each cow dramatically, and at the same time use automated milking methods that increase their productivity. For this reason most countries in the industrial world produce far more milk than they can consume.

Dairy cows can bear calves, and therefore produce milk, when they are about two years old. They will bear three or four calves during their milking lives, then they will have to be replaced by younger animals.

(below) Dairy farms are traditionally quite small and usually located in areas where natural rainfall produces lush grassland. This picture is of Lancashire (England).

(above) With a cow weighing half a tonne and producing 20–40 kg of milk each day, cattle will need to eat their way through huge quantities of food. Traditionally, dairy cattle are allowed to graze on rich pastures during the day, and brought to milking parlours twice a day. However, cattle with such high yields need more energy than the grass alone can provide, so during milking time the cattle are fed high-energy foodstuffs (known as 'concentrates'), often based on cereals and containing extra vitamins and minerals.

During seasons when grass is not growing, the cattle are fed on hay (dried grass) or silage (fermented grass and other chopped up leaves and stalks) which are harvested from ungrazed fields each year.

Breeding dairy cattle such as the Holstein-Friesians, Jerseys and Guernseys allows farmers to collect up to four times as much milk as from a beef cow. A dairy cow can produce 8–12 tonnes of milk per animal per year. It may produce over 90 tonnes during its life, but only if each cow is individually cared for. As a result, dairy farming involves much more labour than beef farming.

In places where the winters are harsh, it is impossible to leave dairy animals out in the cold; they have to be kept inside in barns in separate stalls called mangers. In the past, animals and farmers shared the same large building to help keep each other warm.

To help mechanise dairying, computers and sensors have been introduced to some farms so that a necklace worn by each cow has an identification tag that automatically tells a computer the amount of concentrates to supply to their feeding troughs.

Selective breeding began in Britain in the 18th century. By choosing cattle for particular environments or the products they could be used for, quite distinctive breeds were produced.

> Sheep and goats are the preferred choice for many farmers with dry, wet or cold climates, where soil is poor or where little space is available.

The effects were dramatic. As soon as cattle ranges were enclosed and breeding could be more controlled, specialised breeds, such as Hereford and Angus, replaced the general animals.

This is why few Texas Longhorns survive today

Specialisation has created two distinctive types of animal: those suited to yielding milk and those which put on weight quickly and can be used for beef.

Sheep and goats

Sheep and goats are much smaller and hardier than cattle and they can survive in a wide range of environments. They are therefore the preferred choice for many farmers with dry, wet or cold climates, where soil is poor or where little space is available.

In the industrial countries sheep are either fattened on high-quality pastures for meat (lamb) production, or grazed and their wool harvested each year.

Goats, which have an extraordinary ability to turn even the lowest quality grass or shrubs into meat and milk, cost almost nothing to rear and so are found over much of the developing world, in cities as well as the countryside.

The main commercial wool-producing areas are the drylands of the world, including the outback of Australia, the steppes of the former USSR and the semi-arid regions of the southwestern United States.

World sheep rearing

Of the one billion sheep raised worldwide, Australia raises the most, followed by the former USSR, China, New Zealand, India, and Turkey. Sheep yield about three million tonnes of wool. Most of the international trade in sheep products is from Australia and New Zealand.

Over 300 breeds of sheep occur in the world, but most sheep belong to just a few breeds. The fine-wool breeds are dominated by the Merino and Rambouillet. Medium-wool breeds are dominated by the Cheviot and Southdown; they are also good breeds for meat production. Long-wool breeds include the Leicester.

◻ (above and right) Normally sheep wander freely over rangeland. When sheep are brought together, as in this Australian market, you can see the enormous number of animals involved.

These animals will be sold and will either move to another farm or be slaughtered for meat.

❏ right) The sheep can wander freely over large areas of range, such as here in Australia, seeking out the best plants from the landscape. They are only brought together and kept in pens for shearing, lambing or sale.

Sheep and transhumance

Sheep are vital to many mountain farmers. In this picture a farmer from Kashmir (India) is moving his herd to fresh grazing in the Himalayan mountains at about 5000 m above sea level. These upper level grazing lands are only available for a few short summer months and then the animals have to be taken back to lowland pens. In the meantime, however, the valley fields can be harvested for hay, providing food for the animals during the winter.

The movement of farm animals between lowland and mountains each year is known as transhumance. It was once a way of life for many farmers in European mountain areas, but is so no longer.

❏ (right) The majority of the world's sheep is kept to produce wool. Shearing is still done by hand, often using teams of contract shearers who move from farm to farm. Attempts to automate the shearing have so far met with failure.

❏ (right) Sheep being herded through the high Himalayas.

The main meat-producing areas, by contrast, are where there is high-quality grazing. Countries with a humid climate, such as New Zealand, are important for meat-lamb production.

Pigs

Pigs were first domesticated from wild boars in China about 9000 years ago. As wild animals, boars scavenge on forest floors, eating a wide range of fruits that have fallen from trees or edible roots that grow just below the surface.

Pigs can eat partly decaying material, which has made them an attractive choice of livestock in many parts of the world. However, since their original forest habitat has been destroyed,

> Pigs are widely reared and provide essential protein to much of the developing world.

and since pigs are not grazing animals, they can no longer feed themselves independently. They need to be provided with a source of food by farmers.

Pigs will eat farm and domestic waste, and they can therefore be reared successfully by farmers with very small amounts of land or money in the developing world. However, they grow fastest and most successfully when reared on cereal crops.

Landrace is a popular pork breed in Europe and North America; whereas breeds such as the Large Black are reared for bacon. Pigs intended for bacon are normally reared on dairy by-products; they form an important diary-pig industry in countries such as Germany and Denmark.

Poultry

There are many kinds of farm poultry including chickens, turkeys, ducks and geese. Chickens are the most important of these, providing meat, eggs and feathers.

Like pigs, poultry are easily reared by small farmers with very little money and they

'Yard' animals

Yard farming refers to keeping animals in or about the farmyard. The normal yard animals are chickens and pigs. Modern industrial methods of production mean that nowadays animals are kept in special buildings.

Chickens and pigs are found throughout the world but they are most valuable in most developing world countries. They are valuable because they will eat scraps, they are not prone to wander and need virtually no looking after. Thus they are cheap to maintain, yet they provide meat and, in the case of chickens, eggs.

❒ (above) Traditionally chickens have been allowed to run free and live in small coops. This way of keeping chickens is shown above. It is called free range.

However, the majority of chickens reared for modern supermarkets are not free range. Instead they are kept in much more crowded indoor conditions. Chickens designed for meat live just two months before they are slaughtered. This results in perhaps ten billion broilers being produced each year.

Because chickens raised this way mature faster for less food than any other form of farm animal, their meat is cheaper and therefore in great demand. Many poultry farms are closely associated with supermarket chains, and the chickens are sent directly to the shops after slaughter.

❐ (above and right) Pigs are intelligent, clean and solitary animals; they wallow in mud to cool themselves and to get rid of parasites rather than because they do not choose to keep clean.

Because they are not herd animals, they are best farmed in controlled conditions such as in pens and small fields, rather than being allowed to wander freely across hillsides or rangeland.

In the industrial world most pigs are kept on specialised pig farms, and fed a diet of high-energy cereals; hence they are found in cereal growing areas such as the downs of England or the Corn Belt of the United States.

Many specialist pig farms use sheds or feedlots to keep their animals.

Turkeys
These birds are native to North America and have been imported back to the Old World. Turkeys are allowed to mature until they weigh several kilogrammes. This takes about four months in conditions like those used for chickens. The main markets for turkeys are the United States, Canada and the United Kingdom.

provide an essential source of food for many farms in the developing world. They also fit well into general or mixed farming systems. However, the commercial production of eggs and meat in the industrial world has become a form of factory farming. The birds are kept in small cages on racks inside large sheds (for egg production) or close together on the ground in broiler (meat) production.

Fish

Fish farming is a very ancient technique, and collecting fish (mainly carp) from the paddy field and irrigation canals of irrigated rice areas is still regarded by many East Asian farmers as a natural part of their farming.

So far the best progress has been made with shellfish – prawns shrimps, lobsters, scallops, oysters, clams, crabs, crawfish and mussels. Of the free-swimming fish, catfish, salmon and trout have been reared successfully for many years.

Coastal ponds have been developed in places as far apart as Ecuador, China, Taiwan and Indonesia.

Unusual animals

Farming can be adapted successfully to wild animals as well. Many wild animals are better than domesticated animals at using the food in the natural environment. Thus in Africa, where cattle often suffer from disease, there are farms that now rear wildebeest, zebra and antelope for meat. Such farming is also important for helping to conserve these animals.

However, natural hunting animals like mink and crocodile, are among the most threatened species. Farming these animals for their fur, hides and meat has proved to be the most successful way of reducing the poaching of animals in the wild. It also provides the furs and hides that are so valued. It is likely that farming threatened species will become more popular in the future.

❐ (below) Crocodile farming in Australia.

Glossary

AGE OF DISCOVERY
This began in 1415, when Western Europeans, beginning with the Portuguese, explored the Atlantic Ocean. The most famous of the explorers was Christopher Columbus who sailed on August 3, 1492, from Spain and landed on October 12, 1492, in the Bahama islands.

AQUIFER
A buried rock that can provide enough water to supply a spring or well continuously over many years.

DEVELOPING WORLD
Countries where the majority of people still depend on farming for their living, where wages are poor and where there is a lack of advanced technology such as electricity. There are 125 countries classified by the United Nations as coming into this category, including most of those in Asia, Africa and South America.

EVAPORATION
The loss of water from plants, lakes, flooded land, etc. The rate of evaporation may be high in places where the air is dry and hot.

INDUSTRIAL REVOLUTION
The time, beginning in the 18th century and lasting through the 19th century, when the use of Machines and mass production became the common way of making goods.

MALNUTRITION
When a person has a poor diet they may not have much energy or strength to do normal work. They may also be more prone to disease than normal. People who do not get enough of the right foods to eat are said to be malnourished and they suffer from malnutrition.

SUBSIDY
Governments sometimes have to make food available to their people at a lower price than farmers can afford to produce it. When governments pay for this difference they are subsidising food. The majority of the world's governments subsidise food.

TECHNOLOGY
The way that people make use of scientific discoveries to produce things that people find of value.

Further reading

This book is one of a series that covers the whole of geography. They may provide you with more information. The series is:

Index

World Geography **People** *of the world, population & migration* **Homes** *of the world & the way people live* *The world's* **shops** *& where they are* **Cities** *of the world &* *changing* **energy** *supplies* *The world's* **environment** *& conservation* *World* **weather,** *climate & climatic change* *The* **Earth** *& its changing surface* *World Geography* *travel & communications* **Farms** *& the world's food supply* *World* **industry** *& making goods* *The world's* **resources** *& their exploitation* *The world's changing* **energy** *& migration* **Homes** *of the world & the way people live* *The world's* **shops** *& where they are* **Cities** *of the world & their future* *World* **transport,** *travel & communication* *& conservation* *World* **weather,** *climate & climatic change* *The* **Earth** *& its changing surface* *World Geography* **People** *of the world, population & migration* **Home** *supply* *World* **industry** *& making goods* *The world's* **resources** *& their exploitation* *The world's changing* **energy** *supplies* *The world's* **environment** *& conservation* *live* *The world's* **shops** *& where they are* **Cities** *of the world & their future* *World* **transport,** *travel & communications* **Farms** *& the world's food supply* *World* **indus** *change* *The* **Earth** *& its changing surface* *World Geography* **People** *of the world, population & migration* **Homes** *of the world & the way people live* *The world's* **sho** *resources* *& their exploitation* *The world's changing* **energy** *supplies* *The world's* **environment** *& conservation* *World* **weather,** *climate & climatic change* *The* **Earth** *of the world & their future* *World* **transport,** *travel & communications* **Farms** *& the world's food supply* *World* **industry** *& making goods* *The world's* **resources** *& their* *Geography* **People** *of the world, population & migration* **Homes** *of the world & the way people live* *The world's* **shops** *& where they are* **Cities** *of the world & their fut* *energy* *supplies* *The world's* **environment** *& conservation* *World* **weather,** *climate & climatic change* *The* **Earth** *& its changing surface* *World Geography* **People** *communications* **Farms** *& the world's food supply* *World* **industry** *& making goods* *The world's* **resources** *& their exploitation* *The world's changing* **energy** *supplies* *Th* **Homes** *of the world & the way people live* *The world's* **shops** *& where they are* **Cities** *of the world & their future* *World* **transport,** *travel & communications* **Farms** *&* *World* **weather,** *climate & climatic change* *The* **Earth** *& its changing surface* *World Geography* **People** *of the world, population & migration* **Homes** *of the world &* *industry* *& making goods* *The world's* **resources** *& their exploitation* *The world's changing* **energy** *supplies* *The world's* **environment** *& conservation* *World* **weathe** *world's* **shops** *& where they are* **Cities** *of the world & their future* *World* **transport,** *travel & communications* **Farms** *& the world's food supply* *World* **industry** *& m* *The* **Earth** *& its changing surface* *World Geography* **People** *of the world, population & migration* **Homes** *of the world & the way people live* *The world's* **shops** *& wh* *& their exploitation* *The world's changing* **energy** *supplies* *The world's* **environment** *& conservation* *World* **weather,** *climate & climatic change* *The* **Earth** *& its chan* *& their future* *World* **transport,** *travel & communications* **Farms** *& the world's food supply* *World* **industry** *& making goods* *The world's* **resources** *& their exploitatio* **People** *of the world, population & migration* **Homes** *of the world & the way people live* *The world's* **shops** *& where they are* **Cities** *of the world & their future* *Worl* *supplies* *The world's* **environment** *& conservation* *World* **weather,** *climate & climatic change* *The* **Earth** *& its changing surface* *World Geography* **People** *of the world,* **Farms** *& the world's food supply* *World* **industry** *& making goods* *The world's* **resources** *& their exploitation* *The world's changing* **energy** *supplies* *The world's* **env** *of the world & the way people live* *The world's* **shops** *& where they are* **Cities** *of the world & their future* *World* **transport,** *travel & communications* **Farms** *& the world* *weather,* *climate & climatic change* *The* **Earth** *& its changing surface* *World Geography* **People** *of the world, population & migration* **Homes** *of the world & the way* *& making goods* *The world's* **resources** *& their exploitation* *The world's changing* **energy** *supplies* *The world's* **environment** *& conservation* *World* **weather,** *climate &* *& where they are* **Cities** *of the world & their future* *World* **transport,** *travel & communications* **Farms** *& the world's food supply* *World* **industry** *& making goods* *& its changing surface* *World Geography* **People** *of the world, population & migration* **Homes** *of the world & the way people live* *The world's* **shops** *& where they a* *exploitation* *The world's changing* **energy** *supplies* *The world's* **environment** *& conservation* *World* **weather,** *climate & climatic change* *The* **Earth** *& its changing sur* *future* *World* **transport,** *travel & communications* **Farms** *& the world's food supply* *World* **industry** *& making goods* *The world's* **resources** *& their exploitation* *The u* *of the world, population & migration* **Homes** *of the world & the way people live* *The world's* **shops** *& where they are* **Cities** *of the world & their future* *World* **transpo** *The world's* **environment** *& conservation* *World* **weather,** *climate & climatic change* *The* **Earth** *& its changing surface* *World Geography* **People** *of the world,* **Farms** *& the world's food supply* *World* **industry** *& making goods* *The world's* **resources** *& their exploitation* *The world's changing* **energy** *supplies* *The world's* *of the world & the way people live* *The world's* **shops** *& where they are* **Cities** *of the world & their future* *World* **transport,** *travel & communications* **Farms** *& the worl* *weather,* *climate & climatic change* *The* **Earth** *& its changing surface* *World Geography* **People** *of the world, population & migration* **Homes** *of the world & the way* *& making goods* *The world's* **resources** *& their exploitation* *The world's changing* **energy** *supplies* *The world's* **environment** *& conservation* *World* **weather,** *climate &* *& where they are* **Cities** *of the world & their future* *World* **transport,** *travel & communications* **Farms** *& the world's food supply* *World* **industry** *& making goods* *& its changing surface* *World Geography* **People** *of the world, population & migration* **Homes** *of the world & the way people live* *The world's* **shops** *& where they a* *exploitation* *The world's changing* **energy** *supplies* *The world's* **environment** *& conservation* *World* **weather,** *climate & climatic change* *The* **Earth** *& its changing sur* *future* *World* **transport,** *travel & communications* **Farms** *& the world's food supply* *World* **industry** *& making goods* *The world's* **resources** *& their exploitation* *The u* *of the world, population & migration* **Homes** *of the world & the way people live* *The world's* **shops** *& where they are* **Cities** *of the world & their future* *World* **transpo** *The world's* **environment** *& conservation* *World* **weather,** *climate & climatic change* *The* **Earth** *& its changing surface* *World Geography* **People** *of the world, popu* **Farms** *& the world's food supply* *World* **industry** *& making goods* *The world's* **resources** *& their exploitation* *The world's changing* **energy** *supplies* *The world's* **env** *of the world & the way people live* *The world's* **shops** *& where they are* **Cities** *of the world & their future* *World* **transport,** *travel & communications* **Farms** *& the worl* *weather,* *climate & climatic change* *The* **Earth** *& its changing surface* *World Geography* **People** *of the world, population & migration* **Homes** *of the world & the wa* *& making goods* *The world's* **resources** *& their exploitation* *The world's changing* **energy** *supplies* *The world's* **environment** *& conservation* *World* **weather,** *climate &* *& where they are* **Cities** *of the world & their future* *World* **transport,** *travel & communications* **Farms** *& the world's food supply* *World* **industry** *& making goods* *& its changing surface* *World Geography* **People** *of the world, population & migration* **Homes** *of the world & the way people live* *The world's* **shops** *& where they a* *exploitation* *The world's changing* **energy** *supplies* *The world's* **environment** *& conservation* *World* **weather,** *climate & climatic change* *The* **Earth** *& its changing sur* *future* *World* **transport,** *travel & communications* **Farms** *& the world's food supply* *World* **industry** *& making goods* *The world's* **resources** *& their exploitation* *The u* *of the world, population & migration* **Homes** *of the world & the way people live* *The world's* **shops** *& where they are* **Cities** *of the world & their future* *World* **transpo** *The world's* **environment** *& conservation* *World* **weather,** *climate & climatic change* *The* **Earth** *& its changing surface* *World Geography* **People** *of the world, popu* **Farms** *& the world's food supply* *World* **industry** *& making goods* *The world's* **resources** *& their exploitation* *The world's changing* **energy** *supplies* *The world's* **en** *of the world & the way people live* *The world's* **shops** *& where they are* **Cities** *of the world & their future* *World* **transport,** *travel & communications* **Farms** *& the worl* *weather,* *climate & climatic change* *The* **Earth** *& its changing surface* *World Geography* **People** *of the world, population & migration* **Homes** *of the world & the wa* *& making goods* *The world's* **resources** *& their exploitation* *The world's changing* **energy** *supplies* *The world's* **environment** *& conservation* *World* **weather,** *climate &* *& where they are* **Cities** *of the world & their future* *World* **transport,** *travel & communications* **Farms** *& the world's food supply* *World* **industry** *& making goods* *& its changing surface* *World Geography* **People** *of the world, population & migration* **Homes** *of the world & the way people live* *The world's* **shops** *& where they a* *exploitation* *The world's changing* **energy** *supplies* *The world's* **environment** *& conservation* *World* **weather,** *climate & climatic change* *The* **Earth** *& its changing sur* *future* *World* **transport,** *travel & communications* **Farms** *& the world's food supply* *World* **industry** *& making goods* *The world's* **resources** *& their exploitation* *Tl*